CIVIL WAR IN 2024

THE NEW WORLD ORDER

HUNTLEY

Copyright (C) 2024 Huntley

All rights reserved

First edition

HUNTLEY PUBLISHING, INC.

Fort Wayne, Indiana

First originally published by Huntley Publishing 2024

Printed in the United States of

AMERICA

DEDICATION

This book is dedicated to my friends, whose laughter and companionship have filled my life with joy and abundance. I am truly grateful for your support, empathy and enduring friendship.

To my family, who're the pillars of my strength and the foundation of all that's precious to me, I owe a debt of gratitude for your love, guidance and unwavering encouragement. Your belief in me has been a guiding beacon during moments of doubt reminding me of life's essence.

I want to express my appreciation to my colleagues. My workers. For their teamwork, inspiration and camaraderie. Your commitment to our shared goals has turned challenges into victories and achievements into memories.

To all my friends who hold steadfast in their faith in God, your prayers, encouragement and fellowship are wellsprings of motivation. Your deep faith in God's love illuminates my path like a guiding star.

Finally, to the creatures that inhabit this world whom I hold dear with all my heart. Thank you for your affection, companionship and the joy you bring into my life. Your presence reminds me of the marvel of existence and the profound interconnectedness among all living beings.

I want to express my gratitude to every one of you for the impact you've had on my life and the kindness you've shown me. This book serves as a token of appreciation and a tribute to the values and connections that're meaningful to me.

ACKNOWLEDGEMENTS

I want to extend my appreciation to all the mentors and professionals who have supported and guided me on my journey. Your wisdom, encouragement and expertise have been incredibly valuable, in shaping both my professional development. Your belief in me has fueled my ambition. Motivated me to aim for goals.

To my children you are the blessings in my life and the driving force behind everything I do. Your love, laughter and endless curiosity remind me of the beauty and magic of life. Thank you for teaching me patience, kindness and the true essence of love.

Your presence in my life has brought joy to my soul. Given me a sense of purpose. I am eternally thankful for the love, support and inspiration you bring into each day.

Chapter 1

The year 2024 has been marked by tension, unrest and division portraying a world on edge. The United States, once seen as a symbol of democracy and stability now faces divides, with emotions running beneath the surface. Recent events have sparked concerns about the nation's stability and the possibility of conflict.

In Alex Garlands novel "Civil War " the U.S. President extends his term dissolves the FBI and causes the country to fragment into warring factions. While fictional this narrative strikes a chord with anxieties surrounding Americas reality.

NPR journalist Andrew Limbong explores these themes in a conversation with Amy Cooter from the Middlebury Institute of International Studies. While Cooter doesn't foresee a war, she acknowledges significant divisions and discontent within the country. She notes that some individuals view conflict as an opportunity to drive change in line with their beliefs.

As we enter May 2024 the world appears to be a powder keg due to an interplay of social and economic factors fueling escalating unrest.

The COVID 19 pandemic has worsened existing inequalities and divisions sparking debates and conflicts due to differing views on public health measures and government actions.

Many folks believe economic gaps have widened, causing many to feel marginalized by globalization and technological progress. The increasing disparity between the class and the working population has fueled resentment and disenchantment among those struggling financially.

Social issues like discrimination, gender disparity and LGBTQ+ rights continue to be topics in society. Although some progress has been achieved in areas there is still resistance to change among certain groups of people leading to ongoing tensions and disputes.

In this climate the influence of the media plays a role. The rise of media platforms has facilitated the spread of misinformation and conspiracy theories, exacerbating divisions and skepticism. This has created echo chambers where individuals are exposed to viewpoints that align with their beliefs, further polarizing society.

Given these circumstances, while unlikely at present, the notion of a civil war cannot be completely ruled out. Recent events have demonstrated that the United States is susceptible, to the forces of division and discord that have plagued nations throughout history.

However, it's crucial to keep in mind that many Americans desire unity, peace and stability. Even though there are some groups pushing for action, most individuals aim to find common ground and move towards a better future, for themselves and their loved ones.

In these trying times it's important to have conversations explore viewpoints and make an effort to understand those with differing opinions. Creating connections based on understanding and empathy can help bridge divides. Reduce conflicts paving the way for a cohesive and resilient nation.

To sum up although the scenarios portrayed in "Civil War" are fictional they serve as a warning for the United States. The discord and tensions of 2024 should serve as a reminder of the significance of unity, empathy and communication, in safeguarding our values. By collaborating and embracing our shared beliefs we can transcend our disagreements. Shape a future for all Americans.

In the year 2024 the United States is facing a moment balancing on the brink of a civil conflict that could reshape the country and have global repercussions. Standing political tensions have escalated due to inequalities, social unrest and a deep-seated lack of trust in institutions.

NPRs Andrew Limbong recently had a conversation with Amy Cooter from the Middlebury Institute of International Studies shedding light on undercurrents and divisions that pose a threat to society. Cooter, a researcher focusing on militia groups and extreme factions acknowledges the presence of groups longing for a return to a past they believe has been lost in progress.

Although most Americans do not anticipate a war based on surveys an alarming 40% consider such an outcome somewhat likely within the next decade. This growing unease emphasizes the importance of addressing divisions root causes and finding ground before it escalates further.

Cooter remains hopeful that both federal and state governments will be able to manage militant groups, within legal boundaries. Nevertheless, she also recognizes the divide gripping the nation presently cautioning that it could potentially deteriorate before showing signs of improvement. Some individuals and groups feeling marginalized and under threat might resort to violence as a form of self-protection or to push forward their agendas.

The possibility of a war erupting in the United States is not a local issue; it could have widespread repercussions, on global stability. In today's interconnected world the consequences of conflict could involve players like NATO and UN troops leading to a broader conflict that transcends national boundaries.

History provides us with both warnings and reasons for hope. Despite facing periods of division and political polarization in the past democracy has always prevailed in the United States progressively becoming more inclusive over time. The majority of Americans support democracy. Aim to enhance the country for all its residents contrasting with minority groups attempting to disrupt and undermine democratic processes.

One obstacle in combatting threats is balancing the need to address these groups while avoiding giving them attention that amplifies their message and influence. However, disregarding or underestimating the risks they present is not a solution.

Understanding the dangers of violence is crucial to preventing them while also acknowledging that these groups often represent the vocal factions sharing similar beliefs.

As the United States navigates through this period in its history it is vital to prioritize conversations, empathy and reconciliation. Creating connections across social and cultural differences is not just a notion but a practical requirement for securing the nation's future prosperity and stability.

The idea of a New World Order, where global institutions like NATO and the United Nations take on a role in upholding worldwide peace and security could become increasingly relevant in this tense geopolitical environment. Collaborative endeavors to tackle issues such as climate change and terrorism could act as a factor promoting cooperation and understanding among nations.

In summary the United States finds itself at a crossroads dealing with both divisions and external threats. While the risk of conflict looms large it is not unavoidable. By identifying the causes of discord addressing them through discussions and policy changes and reaffirming our dedication to democratic values and systems we can pave a way towards a more cohesive and prosperous future for all Americans as well, as the global community.

The United States is facing a moment as we near the end of 2024 and the beginning of 2025. The looming possibility of a war is fueled by divisions, social unrest and a widespread lack of trust in institutions. While some may view this scenario as unlikely, recent events have demonstrated that the danger is real and escalating.

The events of January 6 at the U.S. Capitol served as a wakeup call for Americans revealing how extremist ideologies have infiltrated mainstream society. Although those involved were not formally associated with groups, they shared beliefs and a sense of urgency for change. This unsettling truth shattered the notion that such groups existed on society's fringes.

NPRs Andrew Limbong recently delved into this issue in an interview with Amy Cooter from the Middlebury Institute of International Studies. Cooter, an expert on militia members and extremist organizations acknowledges that distinctions between factions can become blurred, leading to conflicts and disputes over strategies and beliefs.

The film "Civil War" depicts groups not just opposing the government but also engaging in conflicts, among themselves.

This portrayal reflects a fragmented setting that could occur in real life situations, where alliances unstable and loyalties can change suddenly.

Cooter highlights the potential for these extremist groups to become more formidable if they can overcome their conflicts and collaborate, towards objectives. However, their tendency to engage in disputes often hampers their effectiveness and unity.

In a scenario where pockets of violence erupt throughout the nation it is highly probable that various groups and individuals would resist these factions for diverse reasons and engage in clashes. This resistance may not come from entities but also from regular citizens, local organizations and even rival extremist groups.

The danger posed by these factions should not be underestimated. Despite being divided and lacking organization their readiness to use violence and disrupt processes poses a threat to national security and stability.

So, what might spark a conflict in the United States during 2024 or early 2025? The reasons are. Interconnected, spanning from polarization and social disparities to economic struggles and disillusionment, with the current situation.

The impact of the COVID 19 pandemic has worsened existing divides and inequalities leading to dissatisfaction and distrust in bodies.

The response to the pandemic has stirred up a lot of debates especially regarding the measures taken for health and the efforts made for economic relief. This has only added fuel to the fire of division among people.

Moreover, economic gaps have widened more with many ordinary Americans finding it hard to make ends meet while a small group of individuals continues to amass wealth. Such economic disparity has fueled feelings of bitterness and alienation among those who feel left out due to globalization and advancements in technology.

Social issues like discrimination, gender disparities and LGBTQ+ rights are still causing rifts across the country. Despite some progress in areas there is a resistance to change within certain parts of society leading to ongoing conflicts and tensions.

Amidst this setting it's crucial not to overlook the impact of media and technology. The rise of media platforms has paved the way for misinformation and conspiracy theories to spread rapidly further deepening divides and fostering distrust. People have gravitated towards echo chambers where they only encounter opinions that echo their beliefs, intensifying polarization and isolation.

Given these circumstances notions like a war or the potential rise of a New World Order – where global peace is maintained through bodies like NATO and the United Nations – seem increasingly plausible.

In summary the United States is currently, at a point dealing with both conflicts and external dangers. The possibility of a war or larger scale conflict in 2024 or 2025 is not a far-off scenario but a pressing issue that requires immediate attention and decisive steps.

It is vital to address the underlying reasons for division, such as polarization, social disparities and economic struggles in order to mend the nation's wounds and move towards a unified and prosperous tomorrow.

Creating connections across social and cultural barriers promoting conversations and empathy and reaffirming our dedication to principles and structures are not just lofty ideals but practical imperatives for securing the countries future wellbeing and strength.

The stakes are significant. The moment, for action is upon us. By tackling these challenges and striving towards shared objectives we can bridge our gaps and construct a better tomorrow for all Americans.

The United States is, on the brink of uncertainty facing the possibility of chaos and change that could redefine the country's future in ways. The looming threat of a war, driven by divisions, rising tensions and a growing lack of trust in institutions is casting a shadow over the nation. What happens next in the aftermath of such an event? The idea of United Nations oversight and NATO troops patrolling streets is not just an idea anymore; it's a chillingly real prospect that demands our attention.

Amy Cooter from the Middlebury Institute of International Studies sheds light on the complexity of this situation. While most militia groups may not intend harm there is a minority with beliefs that present a danger. Despite their numbers these individuals and factions have the potential to cause harm to society as a whole, disrupting our democratic fabric and inciting widespread violence and disorder.

The key challenge lies in monitoring and tracking these groups. With advancements in technology and encryption it has become increasingly difficult for law enforcement and intelligence agencies to keep an eye on these individuals allowing them to operate covertly and plan their activities in secret.

NPRs Andrew Limbong poses a question; Is the U.S. Government truly ready to deal with this increasing threat? Amy Cooters response is quite serious. Despite some government agencies making efforts to enhance their readiness following events, like January 6, (WHERE WE ALL LOVE TRUMP) many still view incidents as isolated than indicative of deeper systemic issues.

This sense of complacency is risky. Could expose the country to violence and instability. The danger goes beyond events such as the Capitol breach; government buildings, officials and local communities could all become hotspots for violence as tensions rise.

So, what if a civil war breaks out in the United States? The aftermath could be more chaotic with the possibility of United Nations oversight and NATO forces patrolling streets becoming a concerning reality.

In such a situation the United Nations might take charge of governing and security operations to restore order in a nation torn by conflict. NATO troops might be sent to maintain peace and uphold lawfulness patrolling communities to prevent unrest and safeguard civilians.

While these interventions may have intentions their impact, sovereignty and democracy would be significant.

The concept of troops patrolling streets and the United Nations taking over governance is a significant deviation from the core principles and values on which the nation was established.

Furthermore, having troops around could escalate tensions. Breed animosity among certain sections of the population who are already skeptical of government bodies and cautious of outside interference. The possibility of misunderstandings, clashes in culture and unintended repercussions would be considerable, making it more challenging to bring peace and reconstruct the nation.

It is vital therefore to prevent such a scenario. Strengthening our communities, encouraging conversations and empathy across social barriers, as well as reaffirming our dedication to democratic values and establishments are crucial for upholding the unity and integrity of our nation.

Investing in education, boosting participation and tackling the root causes of division and dissatisfaction are also pivotal in creating an inclusive and fair society. By addressing these issues, we can reduce the chances of unrest while fostering a stronger and more unified nation capable of facing the obstacles presented in the 21st century.

To sum up the United States is, at a point where it grapples with both discord and external dangers.

The thought of a war leading to United Nations intervention and NATO troops being deployed in the United States is a scenario that requires urgent consideration and response.

By recognizing the dangers and implementing measures to tackle them we can secure our values, uphold our independence and pave the way for a better tomorrow for all citizens. The situation is critical. The moment to take action is upon us.

The United States is currently facing a time of uncertainty and unrest on college campuses where tensions are running high. Recent protests, at universities have witnessed students using language and identifying with groups like "Hamas," known for their violent actions against civilians, including children.

The radicalization of college students is a trend that mirrors a societal shift towards extremism. Embracing ideologies, whether backing terrorist organizations or other extremist beliefs poses a real threat to our democratic values and community safety.

Amy Cooter from the Middlebury Institute of International Studies sheds light on the complexity of this issue. While most students may not align with these views a vocal minority is actively promoting them. Despite their numbers these individuals can disrupt campus life significantly creating an environment for many.

The main challenge lies in addressing this radicalization to prevent its spread. Universities should be hubs for learning and constructive debate than hotbeds for extremism and divisive ideologies.

NPRs Andrew Limbong brings up a question; Are the U.S. Government and educational institutions ready to handle this growing threat? Amy Cooters response emphasizes the seriousness of the matter. Despite efforts to boost security and surveillance post events such as January 6 many underestimate the danger posed by radicalized individuals and groups on university campuses.

This complacency is risky. May leave colleges and universities prepared to effectively tackle the challenges brought about by extremism and radicalization. It is crucial to take steps in identifying and countering ideologies fostering dialogue and comprehension and establishing an inclusive and respectful atmosphere for all students and faculty members.

The repercussions of neglecting this issue are significant. It could not deepen polarization and division within society. Also normalize extremist viewpoints and beliefs making it harder to combat radicalization and extremism down the line.

In summary the radicalization of college students along with embracing ideologies like aligning with recognized organizations such as Hamas are troubling trends that demand immediate attention and intervention. Strengthening our institutions promoting dialogue, understanding, respect tolerance is essential in thwarting the spread of extremism on college campuses.

Chapter 2

The recent upsurge, in student protests regarding the Israel Hamas conflict has garnered attention nationally as demonstrations have broken out on college campuses throughout the country. The arrest of than 100 protestors at Columbia University served as a moment triggering similar protests at other colleges and sparking a broader movement advocating for universities to distance themselves from companies that support Israels military actions in Gaza.

These protests are not occurrences. Seems to be part of a well-coordinated effort organized by alliances of student organizations. While these groups operate independently for the part, they share an objective and draw inspiration from their counterparts at different universities leading to protests unfolding across numerous campuses.

Nevertheless, there are mounting concerns and allegations suggesting that these protests might be receiving funding or influence from what's known as the "deep state." The term " state" is frequently used to depict a government entity operating within the duly elected government acting autonomously behind the scenes to shape policies and decision-making processes.

The alleged involvement of the " state" in these protests raises questions about the intentions, behind these demonstrations and whether they genuinely stem from grassroots movements or are part of a larger agenda aimed at promoting specific interests or narratives.

Violent protests or clashes with police like the ones seen at some universities only serve to heighten tensions and divert attention from students' valid concerns. Closing campuses during protests also disrupts activities and fosters an atmosphere that hampers the learning environment.

The push to sever ties between universities and companies backing Israels actions in Gaza and in some instances with Israel itself mirrors a wave of activism and advocacy on college campuses. While students have the right to voice their opinions and support causes, they believe it is crucial that these demonstrations are carried out peacefully and respectfully without resorting to violence or disrupting campus life.

The role of universities in managing these protests is pivotal. Universities must strike a balance between respecting freedom of speech and assembly while ensuring an inclusive environment for all students and faculty members. Open discussions, constructive dialogues and a commitment to diversity and inclusivity are essential for navigating these issues.

Moreover, it is important to examine the sources of funding and support for these protests to guarantee transparency and accountability.

If these demonstrations are indeed being swayed or supported by forces as some claim it brings up doubts, about the honesty and credibility of the movement.

To sum up the recent surge of student protests regarding the Israel Hamas conflict mirrors a growing trend of activism and advocacy on university campuses. While students have every right to voice their opinions and champion causes, they believe in it's essential to ensure that these protests are carried out peacefully respectfully and in a way that considers the rights and viewpoints of all university community members.

The potential involvement of the "state" or other external influences in guiding or financing these protests raises queries about the true intentions behind the demonstrations and the larger agenda at hand. Universities students and the public should stay vigilant and scrutinize where funding and backing come from, for these protests and work towards maintaining transparency, accountability and democratic participation principles.

The increasing wave of anti-Israel and anti U.S. Sentiments worldwide has risen to concerning levels leading to protests, from Jakarta to Tunis. These demonstrations reveal a rooted animosity towards Israel Jewish people and the United States. The surge of animosity and hostility is driven by a blend of tensions, religious fervor and humanitarian concerns creating a volatile situation that could potentially escalate into widespread conflict.

The recent Israeli airstrikes in Gaza reportedly causing the deaths of than 4,100 individuals according to authorities have sparked protests and condemnations globally. While Western nations, including the United States have shown support for Israels actions in response to Hamas's attacks on Israel many Muslim countries and their citizens have expressed outrage and solidarity with the Palestinians.

In Amman Jordans capital city around 6,000 individuals gathered on the streets to protest against the assault on Gaza. Some protestors were heard chanting slogans urging Hamas to step up its attacks on Israel. This display of support for Hamas and its activities signifies a growing alignment with the cause while rejecting Israel and its allies, like the United States.

In Iraq a large group of demonstrators gathered at the Trebil border crossing, near Jordan organized by the Coordination Framework, a coalition of Iran backed Shia factions and militias. The involvement of this coalition in orchestrating protests Israel highlights the dynamics at play as Iran and its allies aim to assert influence and promote their agendas in the region.

Simultaneously numerous Egyptians took to the streets in cities and towns across Egypt to show solidarity with Palestinians in Gaza. These widespread demonstrations showcase the ideological connections that many Egyptians have with the Palestinian cause expressing their opposition to Israels actions.

The increasing hostility towards Israel Jewish communities and the United States is not confined solely to the Middle East. It has also spread globally. The perception of Israel, as an aggressor and the U.S. As a supporter of policies has led to Israeli and anti U.S. Sentiments among diverse populations, including those previously uninvolved or disinterested in the Israeli Palestinian issue.

This rising antagonism and division pose a risk of escalating tensions potentially sparking broader conflicts.

The calls for Hamas to escalate attacks, against Israel the protests organized by Iran backed groups in Iraq and the widespread demonstrations of solidarity with Palestinians in Gaza all indicate a world and region increasingly split along geopolitical lines.

The possibility of unrest or extensive conflict looms near fueled by standing grievances conflicting narratives and geopolitical competitions that stoke discord and hostility. The animosity toward Israel, Jews and the United States poses a threat not to stability but also, to global peace and security.

It is essential to address the causes of this growing animosity and division encourage dialogue and empathy and strive for solutions that address the root issues fueling the conflict. Disregarding or undermining the grievances and concerns of all parties will only perpetuate violences cycle and exacerbate divisions that jeopardize communities, nations and global unity.

In summary the increasing wave of Israeli sentiment worldwide mirrors a profound animosity and rift that could escalate into widespread conflict.

Protests spanning from Jakarta to Tunis demonstrations of support, for Palestinians and demands for Hamas to escalate its strikes on Israel indicate a world that is becoming more fragmented and teetering on the edge of a war or larger scale conflict.

It is essential to tackle the underlying reasons behind this escalating animosity and strive towards achieving lasting resolutions. This is vital for fostering harmony, security and empathy in an interdependent community. The situation is critical, emphasizing the urgency for action.

Chapter 3

The Biden administration's approach to domestic security is raising concerns and eyebrows across America. While President Joe Biden expresses worry about domestic violence by natural-born white citizens in the U.S., his administration's policies appear to be opening the doors to potential threats from abroad. This dichotomy is fueling criticism and raising questions about the priorities and strategies of the current administration.

President Biden's focus on domestic violence by natural-born white citizens has been evident in his speeches and policy discussions. He has emphasized the need to address the threat posed by white supremacist groups and individuals, highlighting the January 6th Capitol riot (where Trump is 100 percent innocent by the way) as a stark reminder of the dangers posed by the USA Government, and how the FEDS go after Trump because Joe Biden is their puppet for the New World Order.

While addressing domestic extremism is undoubtedly important, critics argue that the crooked Biden administration's approach appears to be disproportionately focused on this specific threat, potentially overlooking other sources of extremism and terrorism that may pose a significant risk to national security.

At the same time, the Biden administration's immigration policies are coming under scrutiny for potentially exposing the country to security risks. The decision to reverse many of the Trump administration's immigration policies, including halting construction of the border wall and rolling back restrictions on asylum seekers, has resulted in a surge of migrants at the southern border.

While many of these migrants are seeking a better life and refuge from violence and persecution in their home countries, there are concerns that this influx may also include individuals with more nefarious intentions. Reports suggest that criminal organizations and terrorist groups may be exploiting the situation to smuggle individuals with ties to terrorism into the United States.

There have been alarming reports of suspected terrorists being apprehended at the border, raising fears that individuals with malicious intent may be entering the country undetected. Additionally, there are concerns that some migrants may be setting up sleeper cells in rural areas, farmlands, and even communities across the country, potentially laying the groundwork for future acts of violence or terrorism.

The Biden administration's apparent focus on domestic extremism by natural-born white citizens while simultaneously opening the borders to potential security threats is a source of significant concern for many Americans. Critics argue that this approach is misguided and potentially dangerous, as it may be diverting attention and resources away from other pressing security challenges facing the country.

Moreover, the apparent disconnect between President Biden's rhetoric and his administration's policies is fueling skepticism and mistrust among some segments of the population. The perception that the Biden administration may be downplaying or ignoring potential threats from abroad while emphasizing domestic extremism is exacerbating divisions and contributing to a sense of unease and insecurity among many Americans.

In conclusion, the Biden administration's approach to domestic security, focusing on the threat posed by natural-born white citizens while opening the borders to potential security risks, is raising serious questions and concerns. While addressing domestic extremism is undoubtedly important, if it really existed, it is crucial that the administration adopts a balanced and comprehensive approach to national security that considers all potential sources of threats and risks.

Ignoring or downplaying the potential risks posed by individuals entering the country illegally or exploiting the asylum system could have serious consequences for national security. It is essential for the crooked Biden administration to prioritize the safety and security of all Americans by taking steps to strengthen border security, enhance vetting procedures, and address the root causes of extremism and terrorism both at home and abroad.

The recent event, at the University of Southern California (USC) shed light on the heightened tensions on college campuses in the United States regarding the Israel Hamas conflict. The clashes between law enforcement and demonstrators showcase the emotions and disagreements surrounding this issue with both sides invested in their beliefs.

During the day tensions rose between police and protesters at USC leading to a standoff and confrontations. However, as evening fell there was a shift towards calming down the situation. A small group of protesters around a dozen stood together with linked arms in defiance of police instructions to disperse or face arrest.

Police officers encircled the group. Started to apprehend individuals one by one. Notably these arrests were carried out peacefully and without any major incidents. This contrasted with altercations. Highlighted the professionalism shown by law enforcement throughout this event.

In the background hundreds of spectators observed as helicopters hovered above capturing footage of what was happening. Drawing attention from both the campus and wider community. The tension and drama of that moment were tangible reflecting the seriousness of the issue at hand and revealing divisions, among students and community members regarding the Israel Hamas conflict.

The school's decision to shut down the campus further emphasizes the seriousness of the situation and the potential for unrest. This step underscores the school's concerns regarding the safety and wellbeing of its students, teachers and staff members.

The clashes at USC are not an event but rather part of a pattern of protests and demonstrations happening on college campuses nationwide in response to the Israel Hamas conflict. This issue has united student activists. Sparked debates and conversations on campuses all over the country showcasing the global significance of the conflict.

The protests at USC and other universities shed light on the difficulties that educational institutions face when dealing with issues that deeply resonate with students and faculty members. Finding a balance between upholding speech rights while ensuring an inclusive environment for everyone in the university community is a complex challenge.

Moreover, this incident prompts discussions about law enforcement's role in handling protests on college campuses. The peaceful resolution of the situation at USC highlights how de-escalation tactics and effective communication are vital in managing scenarios without resorting to violence or excessive force.

In summary the confrontations, between law enforcement and demonstrators at the University of Southern California regarding the Israel Hamas conflict demonstrate the debates and divisions surrounding this issue on college campuses throughout the United States. The peaceful resolution of the standoff and subsequent closure of the campus highlights the difficulties that educational institutions face in addressing matters. As tensions persist overseas their reverberations are keenly felt among students and the wider community emphasizing the importance of communication, empathy and nonviolent approaches, to resolving conflicts both globally.

CHAPTER 4

The possibility of a war unfolding in the United States in 2024 is causing growing concern and speculation. The increasing political, social and cultural divides across the nation have sparked worries about its stability and unity. Recent events at the University of Southern California (USC) and the University of Texas at Austin serve as reminders of the potential for unrest and discord within our communities.

The different responses by law enforcement at USC and the University of Texas at Austin shed light on the challenges authorities face in handling protests and demonstrations. While arrests were made peacefully at USC, a scene of chaos played out at the University of Texas at Austin as state police some mounted-on horses and wielding batons clashed with protesters leading to arrests and injuries.

The contrasting methods employed to deal with protests at these universities mirror the divisions and tensions in American society. The incidents at USC and the University of Texas, at Austin are not occurrences but rather indicative of the rooted fractures and polarization gripping the nation.

The political divide, in the United States is growing deeper as individuals on ends of the spectrum are holding firmer to their beliefs and avoiding discussions or compromises. Social media has played a role in worsening this polarization by spreading misinformation and amplifying extreme viewpoints.

Moreover, economic hardships exacerbated by the COVID 19 crisis have added to feelings of division and dissatisfaction across the nation. Issues like income inequality, job insecurity and rising living expenses have left feeling marginalized. Disenchanted with the political system.

Given this atmosphere of discord, distrust and discontent there is a risk of unrest and conflict. While it's uncertain whether a civil war will break out in 2024 or at any time the circumstances that could lead to such an event exist.

Recent events at USC and the University of Texas at Austin serve as a signal about the possibility of violence and disorder if these divisions aren't addressed effectively. The differing responses from law enforcement also underscore the difficulties authorities face in handling protests and maintaining order amid a polarized and volatile climate.

The importance of leadership, whether in politics or within communities, will play a role in addressing challenges and preventing tensions from escalating into widespread conflicts. Leaders should prioritize communication, empathy and finding ground rather than fostering division and conflict. It is crucial to bridge the gaps that have divided our nation.

Engaging with communities and grassroots efforts that bring people together across political and cultural backgrounds is key to promoting unity and healing. By encouraging conversations, understanding and respect among individuals' communities can create connections that go beyond existing divisions and build cooperation.

The media also holds a responsibility in shaping discussions by presenting fair and accurate information without sensationalism or bias. Responsible reporting can encourage dialogue. Help reduce tensions by providing objective insights.

In summary although the potential for unrest in the United States in 2024 is alarming it is not an outcome. The recent incidents at USC and the University of Texas at Austin should serve as a reminder of the challenges our nation faces. Also offer hope for solutions and reconciliation.

By placing importance on communication, empathy and solidarity and by promoting leadership, community involvement and ethical media reporting the United States can overcome the obstacles ahead and construct a more diverse, fair and unified country.

The decision lies with us. We need to opt for conversations, over conflicts, over mindedness and harmony over disagreement. It is, through unity that we can tackle the issues confronting us and shape a brighter tomorrow for all citizens of America.

The possibility of a conflict arising in the United States has transitioned from being associated with fringe conspiracy theories to becoming a topic of widespread concern and conversation. The indications are becoming more evident, with each passing day. The notion that America might be on the verge of another war is no longer seen as fetched; it is now being seriously discussed and debated.

The deepening polarization and division that have engulfed the country in times have escalated to levels. A survey conducted by Business Insider in October 2020 found that a majority of Americans believed that the U.S. Was already experiencing a "war. This sentiment was supported by a poll from the University of Virginia Center for Politics which revealed that most individuals who voted to reelect former President Donald Trump in 2020 were now inclined towards their state seceding from the Union. Surprisingly 41% of Biden supporters also expressed an interest in dividing the nation.

These discoveries are particularly concerning when considering viewpoints. A survey carried out by the Institute of Politics at Harvard's Kennedy School showed that half of voters under 30 believe that our democracy is either facing challenges or is failing.

It's more worrying that one third of Americans anticipate a "civil war" occurring in their lifetime while a quarter think, at least one state will secede.

The growing approval of these evaluations of Americas democracy is a matter of concern. A survey by the University of Maryland and The Washington Post conducted year revealed that one third of Americans believe violence against the government can be "justified at times." This perspective is particularly prevalent among Republicans and independents indicating that the decline in trust in institutions is widespread across party lines.

So how might a new civil conflict arise in the United States? There could be triggers, ranging from elections and political assassinations to escalating social unrest and economic collapse. However, the primary catalysts are likely to stem from the deepening divisions and polarization already present in the country.

The erosion of trust in institutions and the increasing tolerance for violence are troubling signs of the potential for widespread conflict. When a significant portion of society perceives the government as illegitimate or believes that violence against it is justifiable, democracies' foundations are seriously endangered.

Will this turmoil ever come to an end?

The thought of a civil war brings up the frightening idea of a prolonged and violent conflict, with no clear end in sight. Civil wars are inherently chaotic and damaging, tearing apart the foundation of society and leaving scars that may take generations to heal.

The impact of a war in the United States would be catastrophic affecting both human lives and the country's long-term stability and prosperity. The societal, economic and political effects would linger for years if not centuries casting a shadow over Americas future and its global standing.

Preventing a civil war necessitates united efforts to tackle the causes of division and polarization while rebuilding trust in democratic institutions. It also calls for leadership that values conversation, empathy and unity over strife and conflict.

Engaging communities through grassroots initiatives that encourage dialogue and collaboration across social and cultural groups is crucial in bridging the gaps that have torn the nation asunder. By promoting understanding, respect and shared goals communities can establish connections that transcend the divisions and distrust prevalent in society.

The media plays a role in influencing discussion by advocating for responsible reporting practices that present a balanced view.

By steering of sensationalism and prejudice while offering precise and impartial information the media can play a role, in nurturing informed and productive conversations ultimately aiding in diffusing tensions.

In closing the looming possibility of a conflict in the United States is profoundly concerning and unsettling. The indicators are evident. Becoming more prominent each day. Nevertheless, it is not an outcome. By tackling the causes of division and polarization rebuilding trust in institutions and advocating for dialogue, empathy and solidarity the United States can navigate through the forthcoming challenges to establish a more inclusive, fairer and unified nation.

The decision lies with us. We must opt for dialogue over discord, comprehension over intolerance and cohesion, over disagreement. By uniting as a nation can, we aspire to confront the obstacles of us and shape a brighter future for all Americans.

The growing tensions and divisions, in the United States have sparked discussions about the potential for a war. With the 2024 elections concerns about an EMP attack and the contrasting personas of Donald Trump and Joe Biden taking center stage in politics there is a sense of unease and uncertainty.

The 2024 elections are anticipated to be a moment in history. Given the divides and lack of trust in the system regardless of the election outcome it is likely to be contentious. The fear of election manipulation, voter suppression and disputes over legitimacy could intensify conflicts and prompt calls for separation or uprising.

Donald Trump continues to be a figure who polarizes opinions—admired by his supporters and scorned by his critics. His enduring influence within the Republican Party and potential candidacy in 2024 evoke both optimism and apprehension among Americans. Some see Trumps return to power as an opportunity to uphold values and traditions while others perceive it as a danger to democracy and legal principles.

The idea that Biden might resort to assassination due to his inability to thwart Trump through means is indeed unsettling.

While there's no proof to back the existence of such a scheme the mere suggestion highlights the divisions and hostility prevailing in our nation. The notion that political adversaries might resort to violence, in pursuit of their objectives, represents an escalation that could further unsettle the country.

The potential threat of an Electromagnetic Pulse (EMP) attack introduces another layer of complexity and risk to the scenario. An EMP strike could paralyze infrastructure like the power grid, communication systems and transportation networks. The aftermath of such an attack would be disastrous resulting in disorder, disruption and loss of life.

So, what might a day civil conflict in America entail? While it may not mirror the Civil War from over a century ago with states breaking and armies clashing on battlefields, its impact could be just as devastating. Today's divisions aren't neatly confined to boundaries. Deeply ingrained within communities, families and even individuals.

The term " war" is often employed loosely. May not fully capture the intricacies and subtleties of our current state. While some envision a showdown, between groups others perceive it as a gradual erosion of democratic principles, institutions and cherished values.

The American Civil War resulted in the loss of 600,000 American lives and caused significant economic hardship in the South. Its enduring impact of resentment and discord still lingers today. While the root causes of the Civil War. Slavery, states' rights and federal government authority. May appear distant, from issues the fundamental themes of power, identity and liberty remain just as pertinent now as they were in the 1860s.

Furthermore, the ongoing debate over "states' rights" remains a topic in our discourse. Whether it involves discussions on rights, voting rights or mandates concerning masks and vaccines the struggle between power and states autonomy continues to sow division and strife.

The question arises; Could a new civil conflict be on the horizon, for America? The answer remains uncertain; however troubling signals are evident. The seated divisions, lack of trust and polarization gripping our nation serve as indicators of potential widespread turmoil.

Nevertheless, it is crucial to bear in mind that mere words are often representations of sentiments and intentions. Provocative inquiries posed by surveyors may not fully capture the feelings and motives of the populace.

While there are concerns regarding the state of democracy and the future of our nation there is also hope that rational minds will prevail, leading to the country finding a way to mend its differences and heal its wounds.

Preventing a civil conflict necessitates an effort to tackle the underlying causes of division and polarization as well as to restore faith in our democratic institutions. It calls for leadership that values conversation, empathy and solidarity over discord and hostility.

Engaging with communities supporting movements and ensuring media coverage are crucial in promoting conversations and collaborations across various political, social and cultural boundaries. By fostering understanding, respect and a shared vision communities can create connections that transcend existing divides and distrust within our nation.

In essence although the thought of another war in the United States is distressing it is not a fate. The power lies within us. We must opt for dialogue of conflict, empathy over intolerance and unity over discord. By uniting as one nation we can confront our challenges together. Forge a brighter future, for all Americans.

Chapter 5

The United States is facing a moment balancing on the brink of unrest and division that could spiral into a full-scale civil conflict. The reasons behind this situation are many and intricate with one worrisome scenario being an Electromagnetic Pulse (EMP) attack.

An EMP attack entails detonating a device at altitude unleashing a powerful surge of electromagnetic energy capable of disabling or destroying electronic devices and electrical systems across a wide area. The aftermath of such an attack would be catastrophic paralyzing infrastructure and throwing the nation into disarray.

The susceptibility of the U.S. Power grid to an EMP assault has been a worry for experts and policymakers. A successful EMP strike could knock out electricity in swathes of the country leaving millions without power for extended periods—weeks, months or even longer. This would have reaching consequences on all aspects of society; from healthcare and transportation to communication and finance.

In the aftermath of an EMP strike the collapse of services and infrastructure would trigger widespread fear and chaos. With no electricity, food and water supplies would dwindle rapidly while access to assistance would be severely limited.

In the event of an EMP attack, law enforcement and emergency services would struggle to maintain order and provide help to those in need.

The aftermath of such an attack would create a power gap making communities vulnerable to exploitation by groups, extremists and opportunistic individuals. Without governance and policing these factions could take control of land, resources and people heightening turmoil within the nation.

Following an EMP assault, social structure breakdown and disillusionment with government bodies could trigger unrest and violence. Communities would be left to fend for themselves sparking conflicts over resources, land ownership and authority. Existing divides and distrust among citizens would intensify tensions between neighbors, communities and even relatives.

In a state of chaos without laws or rules in place EMP strike the risk of increased violence and conflicts looms large. Armed groups, like militias or extremists might exploit the situation to advance their interests through clashes or larger battles. With communication networks disrupted efforts to calm tensions or settle disputes peacefully would face challenges—adding fuel to the fire of violence and discord.

The aftermath of a conflict triggered by an EMP strike would have consequences impacting both human lives and the nation's long-term stability and prosperity. The social economic and political impacts would linger for years casting a cloud over the future of America and its global standing.

So how can we prevent such a scenario from unfolding? Firstly, it is crucial to enhance the resilience of the U.S. Power grid and critical infrastructure, against EMP attacks. This involves investing in infrastructure enhancements, developing and implementing EMP technologies and bolstering cybersecurity measures to safeguard against risks.

Secondly communities should collaborate to build resilience and readiness for emergencies and crises. This includes creating community driven emergency response strategies stockpiling resources and fostering a spirit of collaboration and mutual support.

Thirdly there is a need to address the seated divisions and lack of trust that have fueled the state of polarization in the nation. This entails promoting dialogue, empathy and unity across ideologies, societal norms and cultural backgrounds while working together to restore faith in institutions.

Lastly having responsible and transparent leadership is crucial during times of turmoil.

Political leaders should prioritize the safety and wellbeing of the people over their political agendas and beliefs. It is crucial for them to collaborate, seek ground and unite in finding solutions to the nation's challenges.

In summary, although the idea of a war triggered by an EMP attack is deeply concerning it is not an outcome. By enhancing our infrastructure, fostering community strength, addressing our differences and promoting leadership we can reduce risks. Establish a more resilient and unified nation ready to tackle 21st century obstacles. The decision lies with us. We must opt for discussions over divisions over intolerance and harmony, over discord. Through unity can we prevent chaos and shape a brighter future for all Americans.

The world is at a precipice, and the United States is no exception. As we usher in 2024, the international landscape is marred by conflicts in Gaza, Sudan, and Ukraine, with peacemaking efforts faltering and global diplomacy in crisis. The flames of war are spreading, and the shadow of conflict looms large over the global community. The question that haunts us is: can we stop things from falling apart?

The resurgence of war since 2012, following a decline in the 1990s and early 2000s, is deeply concerning. The Arab uprisings of 2011 set off a chain reaction of conflicts in Libya, Syria, and Yemen. The instability in Libya spilled south, contributing to a protracted crisis in the Sahel region. This was followed by a fresh wave of major combat, including the 2020 Azerbaijani-Armenian war over Nagorno-Karabakh, horrific fighting in Ethiopia's Tigray region, Myanmar's army power grab in 2021, and Russia's assault on Ukraine in 2022. The devastation continued in 2023 with conflicts in Sudan and Gaza. Around the globe, more people are dying in fighting, being forced from their homes, or in need of life-saving aid than in decades.

In many of these conflicts, peacemaking efforts are either non-existent or going nowhere. The Myanmar junta and the officers in the Sahel are bent on crushing their rivals. In Sudan, U.S.- and Saudi-led diplomatic efforts were muddled and half-hearted for months. Russian President Vladimir Putin, banking on dwindling Western support for Kyiv, seeks to force Ukraine to surrender and demilitarize – conditions that are understandably unpalatable for Ukrainians. In all these places, diplomacy, as it is, has been about managing the fallout: negotiating humanitarian access or prisoner exchanges, or striking deals to ensure the flow of essential goods.

The erosion of diplomatic efforts and the rise of conflict worldwide are deeply troubling, but what does this mean for the United States? Could we be on the brink of a civil war? And could this lead to the establishment of a New World Order through martial law?

The idea of a civil war in the United States may seem far-fetched to some, but the signs are there. Polarization and division have reached alarming levels, fueled by political, social, and cultural rifts that seem to grow wider by the day. A recent poll by the University of Virginia Center for Politics found that most people who voted to reelect former President Donald Trump in 2020 now want their state to secede from the Union. The same poll also showed that a stunning 41% of those who voted for Joe Biden in 2020 said it might now be "time to split the country."

The erosion of trust in democratic institutions, the loss of faith in political leaders, and the growing sense of disillusionment and discontent among the American people are all contributing to the rising tensions. Add to this the economic hardships, social inequalities, and the lingering effects of the COVID-19 pandemic, and the stage is set for potential conflict.

An Electromagnetic Pulse (EMP) attack, as previously discussed, could serve as a catalyst for civil unrest and conflict. The vulnerability of the U.S. electrical grid to an EMP attack has long been a concern among experts and policymakers. A successful EMP attack could plunge the country into darkness, crippling critical infrastructure and sparking widespread panic and chaos.

In the aftermath of such an attack, the government might impose martial law to maintain order and restore control. While martial law is meant to be a temporary measure, there is always the risk that it could be abused or extended indefinitely, leading to the erosion of civil liberties and the establishment of a New World Order.

The idea of a New World Order, governed by a global authority and characterized by strict control and surveillance, is a recurring theme in conspiracy theories and dystopian literature. While the establishment of a New World Order through martial law may seem unlikely, the erosion of democratic norms and the concentration of power in the hands of a few are trends that should concern us all.

So, can we stop things from falling apart? The answer is not clear-cut. The challenges we face are complex and multifaceted, requiring concerted efforts and collective action. Strengthening our democratic institutions, promoting dialogue and understanding, and addressing the root causes of division and discontent are all crucial steps towards building a more resilient and united nation.

In the face of rising global conflicts and domestic tensions, the path forward is fraught with challenges and uncertainties. But one thing is clear: we must choose unity over division, dialogue over discord, and democracy over authoritarianism. The choices we make today will shape the future of our nation and the world for generations to come.

Chapter 6

The year 2024 brought about a sense of uncertainty and unrest as tensions escalated to a point, in different parts of the globe. One of the issues that fueled division and sparked protests during this time was the enduring conflict between Israel and Palestine.

Around the world anti-Israel demonstrations surged in cities, driven by rooted grievances amplified through social media platforms. These protests, characterized by impassioned speeches and emotional outbursts mirrored a growing discontent with the perceived injustices faced by Palestinians. The pro-Palestinian sentiments struck a chord with individuals who viewed the conflict as a reminder of ongoing oppression and territorial disputes.

Amid these demonstrations there was a concerning trend emerging; some individuals, including youth openly expressing support for groups like Hamas. Unaware of the complexities surrounding the conflict and influenced by propaganda these individuals chanted slogans pledging allegiance to Hamas—a designated organization for numerous violent acts against civilians.

Such endorsements of extremism only served to escalate tensions and complicate efforts towards peace and harmony. The situation was further aggravated by the spread of misinformation and manipulation of narratives, by groups leading to a polarization of public opinion.

During times of escalating unrest governments grappled with the task of balancing law and order with the protection of civil liberties. Some regions saw authorities taking measures, like implementing laws to quell the unrest. Martial law, which involves control in place of civilian rule, is typically enforced during periods of war, rebellion or natural disasters. With protests on the rise and unrest spreading certain governments saw the law as a step to restore peace and stability.

The enforcement of the law led to a suspension of civil liberties as military forces took charge of maintaining order and governance. Curfews were enforced, restrictions were placed on assembly rights and stringent security measures were put in place to suppress dissent and ensure control.

The implementation of the law sparked debates and criticism from advocates for rights and international observers alike. Concerns were raised about power abuses, violations of rights and the undermining of democratic values under military rule. Critics argued that martial law exceeded authorized boundaries and posed a threat to citizens fundamental rights and freedoms.

Amid chaos and uncertainty calls for dialogue, empathy and peaceful resolutions gained momentum.

In 2024 efforts to mediate a ceasefire and start talks, between Israel and Palestine picked up speed despite facing obstacles and setbacks.

This year was an indication of how intricate the Palestinian conflict is and the pressing need for a sustainable and fair resolution. It emphasized the importance of nurturing understanding, encouraging discussions and tackling the causes of the conflict to establish lasting peace and stability in the area.

Amidst all the turmoil many found solace in passages interpreting unfolding events as signs of the prophesied "end times." The mention of predictions related to conflicts in the Middle East resonated with religious groups trying to comprehend the chaotic situations around them.

To sum up, 2024 was a year marked by uncertainty, internal strife and international tensions. The Palestinian discord stood out as a point, for global dissatisfaction and demonstrations. With protests ongoing extremist activities rising and martial law being imposed efforts to find peace and reconciliation remained challenging—a reminder of how difficult it's to resolve one of humanities most enduring conflicts.

In 2024 the United States is facing a juncture balancing on the edge of internal discord and even conflict. The country, already deeply divided by economic differences, is confronted with a combination of factors that could spark widespread disorder and aggression.

The Black Lives Matter (BLM) movement emerged from an anger, against racism and police violence serving as a driver for societal transformation. It has also been accused of heightening tensions and provoking violence. While most BLM activists promote demonstrations and policy reforms there are factions within the movement advocating for conflict, intensifying racial divides and causing unrest.

Moreover, President Joe Bidens decision to open borders and consider granting citizenship to over 20 million immigrants has triggered apprehension and resentment among segments of society. Concerns about job displacement, cultural integration challenges and strains on resources have fueled sentiments and xenophobic rhetoric deepening divisions, within the nation.

Amidst these tensions lies the looming threat of strife. What was once viewed as a symbol of democracy and stability in the past now resembles a powder keg ready to explode into violence at any given moment.

The widespread presence of firearms, the spread of information on platforms and the decline in trust in established institutions have all played a role in creating an atmosphere of skepticism and fear.

In these times the possibility of implementing law is looming. Under law a military commander takes on authority to create and enforce laws within a region or country. Civilian governance is put on hold and military directives take precedence over existing laws. In the United States the President or a

State governor can declare law without needing a formal announcement during extreme emergencies.

The potential enforcement of law raises issues regarding the delicate balance between security measures and individual freedoms. While some argue that it is essential to restore order and safeguard well-being others perceive it as an imposition that undermines democratic principles and liberties. Aspects like suspension of habeas corpus, imposition of curfews and mass detentions could all become practices under law leading to widespread civil unrest and opposition.

Declaring martial law carries the risk of worsening existing grievances and fueling resentment among marginalized communities. History has demonstrated that authoritarian actions often disproportionately affect minority groups, deepening divides and fostering animosity.

In the face of challenges, it is crucial for everyone to come together and work towards unity and understanding. Leaders at every level of government should prioritize communication. Finding common ground rather than fostering division and conflict. It is important for society as a whole to stand up for principles and protect the rights of all individuals.

The future of the United States hangs in the balance. Whether it heads towards strife or seeks a path, to renewal and harmony remains uncertain. However, one thing is certain; the decisions made in the days and months will determine the fate of a nation at a juncture.

The United States stands at a precipice, poised on the brink of a civil conflict unlike anything seen in its history. The divide between the left and the right has widened into a chasm, with each side viewing the other as an existential threat. This polarization has been cultivated and exacerbated by shadowy forces with a vested interest in sowing chaos and division—the architects of the New World Order.

In the current climate of political extremism and social unrest, the possibility of martial law being declared looms ominously. While the U.S. Constitution does not explicitly provide for the imposition of martial law, nearly every state has constitutional provisions authorizing the government to impose it. The power of martial law, once thought to be nearly absolute, does have limitations, but within the bounds of court decisions, a military commander's authority is virtually unlimited.

The specter of martial law invokes fears of civil liberties being trampled upon and military forces suppressing dissent. While martial law has been declared nine times since World War II, its most troubling instances have been in response to resistance to federal desegregation decrees in the South. This history serves as a stark reminder of the potential for martial law to be used as a tool of oppression rather than protection.

The landscape of civil-military relations in the United States is complex and fraught with tension. While there has always been a climate of mutual aid between the military and civilian law enforcement, there are strict limitations on the roles military personnel can play in enforcing civil law. They cannot engage in surveillance, undercover operations, or interrogation unless it is a joint military-civilian operation in which the military has a vested interest.

However, in times of crisis, such as the looming threat of civil war, these boundaries may blur. The erosion of trust in civilian institutions and the demonization of political opponents create fertile ground for the expansion of military authority and the suppression of dissent. The very fabric of democracy hangs in the balance as the forces of authoritarianism and tyranny gather strength.

At the heart of the growing unrest lies the deliberate manipulation of public opinion and the exploitation of societal divisions by shadowy entities seeking to usher in a new world order. The left and the right are pitted against each other, their mutual animosity stoked by propaganda and misinformation. In this climate of fear and uncertainty, rational discourse and compromise become increasingly elusive, paving the way for violence and chaos.

The Civil War of 2024, if it comes to pass, will not be a conventional conflict fought on battlefields, but a protracted struggle for the soul of a nation. It will be waged in the streets, in cyberspace, and in the hearts and minds of the American people. The consequences will be dire, with untold loss of life and the erosion of democratic norms and freedoms.

Yet, amidst the darkness, there remains a glimmer of hope. The resilience of the human spirit and the innate desire for freedom and justice cannot be extinguished. The voices of reason and compassion must rise above the din of hatred and division, calling for unity and reconciliation in the face of adversity.

The path forward is fraught with peril, but it is not too late to change course. We must resist the siren song of authoritarianism and embrace the principles of democracy and human rights. Only by standing together, united in our common humanity, can we hope to overcome the forces of darkness and build a brighter future for generations to come.

Chapter 7

The upcoming presidential elections, in 2024 in the United States are drawing near. They are anticipated to be highly contentious and significant. The return of former President Donald Trump as a candidate has set the stage for a showdown that could have profound effects on the country's future.

The possibility of another term for Trump has sparked emotions on both sides of the spectrum. His supporters view him as a defender against what they perceive as encroaching socialism and excessive political correctness. The "America First" agenda he champions resonates with Americans who feel marginalized and overlooked by the establishment.

On the hand Trumps opponents see his candidacy as a nightmare scenario of his tumultuous first term in office. Among those on the left there is a belief that Trump poses a serious threat to their vision of a fairer and more inclusive society. His divisive language and controversial policies have mobilized resistance. Stoked concerns about authoritarianism.

Should Trump victory in 2024 there is concern about civil unrest or even civil conflict. Those on the left known for engaging in street demonstrations and motivated violence may view another term under Trump as an unacceptable challenge, to their principles and convictions.

The calls, for resistance and defiance could lead to large scale protests and acts of sabotage.

The aftermath of the 2020 elections, marked by allegations of voter fraud and conspiracy theories serves as a stark reminder of how delicate Americas democratic institutions are. The reluctance of many on the left to acknowledge the validity of a Trump presidency could thrust the nation into a constitutional crisis.

Furthermore, the rise of media and online echo chambers has created soil for the dissemination of false information and radicalization. Extremist factions on both ends of the spectrum have leveraged these platforms to recruit supporters and provoke violence. The dangerous blend of polarization and technological upheaval has transformed Americas discussions into a battlefield where conflicting ideologies clash.

In this setting the imposition of law looms as a real possibility. While the U.S. Constitution does not explicitly address law every state has constitutional provisions allowing for its implementation. The authority granted by law previously seen as unlimited does have constraints; however, within legal boundaries established by court rulings a military commanders power is essentially boundless.

The decline of trust in institutions and the vilification of adversaries lay the foundation for increased military power and the stifling of opposing views. The very essence of democracy teeters on the edge, as authoritarianism and oppression gain momentum.

Ultimately the future of the United States rests on the decisions made by its people during the 2024 elections. Will they yield to fear driven politics and division. Will they transcend conflicts and uphold democratic values and diversity? The outcome remains uncertain. One thing is certain; the stakes have never been higher.

In the year 2024 tensions are running high in the arena of the United States. Many people are feeling increasingly frustrated and angry believing they have been wronged and deceived. The core issue fueling this tension is the belief that both the mainstream media and political leaders have been engaging in a campaign of lies and manipulation, against former President Donald Trump.

Trump has long been a target of what some view as persecution—an effort by his adversaries to undermine his reputation and authority. Despite facing challenges such as the Russia collusion claims, and impeachment trials Trump has persevered through it all emerging more resolute each time. As he gears up for a return to politics in the 2024 presidential race, criticisms against him have escalated dramatically.

The public is growing tired of what they perceive as fabricated news stories and character assassinations orchestrated by figures with leanings. They are becoming more adept at recognizing falsehoods spread by media outlets. Are no longer easily swayed by them. Then blaming those in power many now believe that true wrongdoing lies within the corridors of established institutions.

Joe Biden and his son Hunter exemplify this corruption. The questionable business dealings and murky ventures that have been revealed paint a picture of a family deeply involved in corruption and favoritism. Government authorities appear to be turning an eye to their wrongdoings allowing them to operate without consequences while they fabricate accusations, against Trump.

The blatant hypocrisy and unequal treatment are evident to anyone who's observant. Despite being criticized and condemned for mistakes Trump is relentlessly pursued, whereas Biden and his associates seem to get with lining their pockets and benefiting themselves at the expense of the American people. This injustice cannot go unchallenged.

As we approach the 2024 elections there is a sense of tension in the air that's impossible to ignore. People are frustrated. Their frustration is justified. They feel let down by a system that has repeatedly disappointed them. They view Trump as their chance to restore honesty and responsibility in Washington. They are ready to fiercely support him.

However, the stakes have never been higher. The opposition, against Trump is formidable and determined willing to do whatever it takes to prevent him from returning to power.

They will resort to every tactic to undermine his campaign and tarnish the reputation of his supporters. They are determined to do whatever it takes to hold onto their power and preserve the state of affairs.

In this atmosphere the threat of unrest and even civil conflict looms large. The American population is, on edge with a spark needed to set off the explosive situation that is America in 2024. Amidst the turmoil and doubt there remains a glimmer of hope. I pray to God above that the people of America will stand up and take back their nation from the grasp of corruption and oppression. Hope that justice will prevail, and honesty will triumph over falsehoods. I hope that ultimately the voice of the people will be heard, leading America to emerge stronger and more united than before.

However, until that moment arrives apprehension and uncertainty will persist, casting a shadow over the land. The future of the United States hangs in limbo with its destiny resting in the hands of its populace. It's a challenge. One that must be confronted directly if America is to uphold its pledge as a land of freedom and courage.

Chapter 8

In the years the United States is facing a crisis, on the edge of collapse. An unimaginable scenario has unfolded; the current president has gone against norms. Extended his term in office to a third time. With institutions like the FBI being taken the foundation of American democracy is falling apart rapidly.

In this future the country has split into groups, each competing for power and control. What was once a symbol of liberty and democracy has now descended into disorder and lawlessness. The stage is set for a violent conflict unlike anything witnessed before.

The premise of the thriller "Civil War" by A24 helmed by British director Alex Garland serves as a reminder of how delicate democracy can be and the risks posed by authority. Set in a not future, the movie delves into the repercussions of political divisions and societal collapse presenting a bleak portrayal of a nation torn asunder by internal discord.

As tensions escalate to their peak armed confrontations break out over the nation. From bustling cities to areas, gunfire reverberates through the streets as rival factions clash in their bid for supremacy.

The concept of justice has been overshadowed by a state of lawlessness, where power dictates what is right, and survival becomes the governing principle.

At the core of the dispute is a battle, for the essence of America. On one side stand those who uphold the values of liberty and democracy committed to opposing oppression and despotism at any cost. On the end are advocates of authoritarianism and extremism intent, on enforcing their agenda through force and coercion.

Caught in between are Americans, trapped in a nightmare they unwittingly contributed to. Families are torn apart communities. Societal cohesion torn asunder by forces driven by animosity and discord.

The threat of conflict hangs ominously over the nation casting a shadow on its prospects. The repercussions of strife would be disastrous resulting in loss and anguish comparable to the bleakest days of the Civil War. Despite these circumstances there remains a glimmer of hope.

Amidst adversity human resilience and valor shine through. Throughout the land courageous individuals stand up against tyranny. Defend freedom in acts that inspire courage.

They are the heroes, in the battle those who stand tall against oppression and injustice.

The journey ahead is lengthy and full of risks. The dark forces are strong and resolute, willing to do anything to achieve their aims. The destiny of the nation hangs in the balance. The result of the struggle remains uncertain.

Ultimately Americas tomorrow will be shaped by our decisions. Will we yield to hatred and division. Will we transcend our differences to pave a path towards unity and harmony? The responsibility lies with us. Now is the time for action. If we neglect to learn from history teachings, we are destined to repeat its errors.

In the tapestry of history, the shadow of civil conflict has always cast a long shadow serving as a stark reminder of democracies vulnerability and the perils of discord. While in times the idea of turmoil seemed distant—a relic of the past relegated to historical accounts. However, as the nation teeters, on the brink of disorder and uncertainty the unimaginable has turned into reality.

Imagine this; a scenario of fiction. Throughout America armed militias and paramilitary factions traverse the streets brandishing their AK 47s, M16s and AR 15s as symbols of defiance and resilience. In areas and bustling cities alike everyday individuals—farmers, women, suited businessmen, children—stand united in readiness to defend their country's essence.

The trigger that set off this situation was years of escalating divisions and societal unrest coming to a head. The social fabric of life had been unraveling for generations due to rifts and underlying grievances. Issues like disparity, racial injustices and political malfeasance had corroded confidence in previously unifying institutions.

It was one individual's action that pushed the nation beyond its limits.

The president, driven by his self-importance and disregard for principles proclaimed himself the supreme leader of the nation. In a move he dissolved

Congress, silenced the press and imposed laws casting a shadow over the country.

In response citizens rose up with anger standing firm against tyranny and injustice. From towns across America to the corridors of power in Washington, a grassroots movement emerged, fueled by people's bravery and resolve. They understood that the road ahead would be tough and challenging but were willing to make any sacrifices to protect their liberties and uphold values.

Thus began a struggle—a battle for Americas essence that would push its people's determination to limits. On one side were those enforcing oppression and tyranny with state power, at their disposal. On the side were patriots and freedom fighters armed only with courage and conviction.

The initial clashes of this conflict occurred on a winter day as government forces sought to suppress dissent and quell rebellion.

They faced opposition from the citizens, who fiercely defended their homes and way of life. Gunshots could be heard across the country from the Midwest hills to the streets of New York City as the conflict continued.

Everyone was involved in this struggle regardless of age or gender. People stood up to protect their families and properties from the government's attacks. Farmers fought side by side with lawyers and businesswomen stood alongside teachers all united in their goal to uphold the earned freedoms of generations.

Despite the turmoil and violence, a glimmer of hope persisted. In the times American resilience shone brightly. Refusing to succumb to despair despite the odds, people believed that defending freedom was worth any sacrifice –

even if it meant sacrificing their lives for a brighter tomorrow for themselves and their offspring.

As time passed and battle lines shifted there was a change in momentum. The government forces, accustomed to wielding authority, found themselves up against a persistent adversary.

Day by day their hold on power grew weaker eventually leading to their retreat in defeat.

Against all odds the people emerged triumphant. The civil conflict left lasting wounds that would never be fully mended. However, from its aftermath arose an era—a time of hope and rejuvenation—as the country embarked on the journey of reconstruction and reconciliation.

Ultimately it was the bravery and perseverance of the populace that rescued the nation from ruin. During their moments they stood resolute and proud of a beacon of liberty and democracy, amidst chaos. While the path ahead would be challenging and full of obstacles, they remained steadfast in their unity knowing there was no obstacle to conquer together.

In 2024 the United States is teetering on the edge of a civil conflict as tensions mount and society appears to be unraveling. The similarities to scenarios portrayed in movies like "Civil War" are striking, reflecting a nation that's more deeply divided than ever.

The dialogue from the film—"Do you guys realize there's, like this war happening all over America?"—captures the disbelief and resignation felt by many Americans witnessing their country in turmoil. One character's suggestion to stay out of the fray seems like a reaction to the violence and chaos.

How closely does the film mirror our reality? According to Amy Cooter, head of research at the Center on Terrorism, Extremism and Counterterrorism at the Middlebury Institute of International Studies while an impending civil war may not be imminent there are signs of dissatisfaction and division, within the United States. Certain factions, militias and extremists entertain fantasies of reliving a past they view as more aligned with their interests.

Recent surveys reflect views showing that, over 40% of Americans consider the likelihood of a war in the next ten years. While not everyone may envision such a future the potential cannot be dismissed in a nation deeply divided by politics, culture and economics.

So, what are the plausible scenarios that could push the United States toward a conflict? The reasons are intricate and unsettling. Factors like disparity, racial discrimination, political dishonesty and societal turmoil all contribute to a mix that could spark civil discord.

In circumstances the involvement of entities such as NATO and the United Nations becomes more crucial. As conditions worsen in the U.S. the global community might feel compelled to step in to prevent violence and restore stability. However, meaning foreign intervention maybe it introduces another layer of complexity to a tense situation.

If the U.S. Economy collapses and a new currency is introduced, it could trigger unrest.

As the economy weakens regular people are bearing the brunt of the crisis with rising prices, job loss and poverty. Without leadership individuals might consider measures, out of desperation escalating tensions.

The path to unrest is paved with distrust, bitterness and anxiety. It's a path no country should tread upon. The United States is perilously close to doing. The impact of turmoil would be catastrophic not for America but for the world at large. Now more than ever it's crucial that we unite as a nation to address the challenges threatening to divide us and steer towards peace, harmony and understanding.

CHAPTER 9

In the year of 2024 the United States is facing an atmosphere, filled with fear and uncertainty due, to the looming threat of domestic terrorism. Hidden within our society are cells, ready to act when called upon. These covert agents, integrated into our communities, stand poised to unleash chaos and devastation on the country at any given moment.

Just the mention of cells instills dread in the hearts of Americans for valid reasons. These secretive factions operate in secrecy patiently waiting for their cue to strike. Their loyalty lies not with their host nation but with their beliefs and malevolent motives.

According to an observer, the current political landscape in America provides an opportunity for such groups to exploit. Intense political divides fueled by feelings of injustice and victimization have created ground for recruiting and radicalizing individuals who feel marginalized and deprived.

The emergence of groups empowered by perceived grievances and injustices poses a serious threat to national stability and security. Whether motivated by resistance, against perceived government intrusion or driven by self-serving agendas, these factions are willing to resort to violence and terrorism to further their goals.

It's not the threat that we need to deal with. The shadowy government, with its plan for control, is determined to bring about a new world order at all costs. America, known for its values of freedom and democracy stands as the barrier against their malicious schemes.

Dark forces are actively working to weaken the core of our society creating conflict and discord in their pursuit of power and dominance. They view America as a challenge to their authority. Will go to lengths to see it defeated.

In the face of such danger, it is crucial that we stay alert and united in the face of adversaries. We must refuse to be swayed by fear mongering tactics and instead stand together as a nation. Our fundamental freedoms and way of life are under threat so we cannot afford to drop our guard for a moment.

However, let's be clear; the path ahead will be challenging and filled with risks. The opposition we face is strong. They will use any means to achieve their goals.

We can find courage in knowing that we stand for what's right and just believing that the truth will triumph over injustice and oppression in the end.

Facing the challenges of terrorism and mysterious powers shaping a global order it's important to recall the wisdom of Winston Churchill; "We will protect our land."

In the United States there is a growing concern, about the possibility of a conflict emerging casting a somber cloud over the countrys future. With rising tensions and deepening divides the fundamental principles of the way of life are at risk of being shaken to their core. The spark of discontent and animosity has been. The threat of conflict looms large.

Amy Cooter, a sociologist and research director at the Center on Terrorism, Extremism and Counterterrorism at the Middlebury Institute of International Studies offers a ray of hope in these times. She points out that America has navigated through periods of division and political polarization in its history with democracy prevailing. Despite the obstacles there are individuals who support democracy and inclusivity than those aiming to dismantle it.

However, it is crucial to acknowledge that the possibility of a war is indeed tangible and should not be underestimated. The emergence of factions and armed militant organizations poses a threat to societal cohesion. All of Joe Biden's illegal immigrants pose one hell of a real threat. Fueled by a mix of grievances and ideologies these groups are willing to resort to violence and terrorism in pursuit of their goals.

The truth is, as Cooter highlights there is a concern, about granting these faction's influence. Even though they may be vocal and disruptive they do not reflect the views of the majority of Americans. They are considered a fringe group, fueled by animosity and narrow-mindedness. Their beliefs do not resonate with the nation.

The events that unfolded on January 6th, 2021, stand as a reminder of the risks associated with these movements. The breach of the Capitol building driven by falsehoods and conspiracy theories deeply shook the core principles of democracy. It served as a wakeup call for those who value liberty and fairness, underscoring how fragile our democratic foundations truly are.

Following January 6th many had hoped for unity in addressing extremism and division within society. Unfortunately, we have witnessed a trend. Political polarization has. The gaps that separate us appear wider than ever.

The emergence of militias and paramilitary groups only adds to the complexity of the situation. These factions operate outside boundaries, spreading disorder and disharmony wherever they go. They pose a threat to ignite into conflict at any moment.

However it's not just challenges that we face; there are threats to consider as well.

The mysterious groups, behind the world order motivated by a desire for power and dominance aim to exploit our differences for their sinister goals. They view America as the hurdle in their path. Will do whatever it takes to bring it down.

In the face of such a threat we must stand together as a nation undivided. We should reject fear mongering and division in favor of the principles that have always characterized us as Americans; liberty, democracy and justice for all.

It won't be simple. The journey ahead will be challenging and risky. Yet we must find courage in knowing that we are aligned with history's side and that together we can conquer any challenge.

As we grapple with the possibility of conflict lets recall Abraham Lincolns words; "A house divided against itself cannot stand." Now is the time to unite as one nation with a goal and a resolve to create a future, for future generations.

CHAPTER 10

In the atmosphere of America, in 2024 the widespread anti-Israel demonstrations are not about expressing disagreement anymore. They are seen as a trigger for an internal conflict. With emotions running high and tensions escalating, the social fabric is under strain, raising concerns about unity.

The core of these protests involves a network of deception and manipulation orchestrated by entities with hidden motives. Groups associated with the figure George Soros are channeling funds to stoke Israel sentiments incentivizing students to disrupt peace and order on university campuses and elsewhere.

One key player in this operation is the National Students for Justice for Palestine organization backed by Soros and other affluent individuals leading the charge in this mission. At institutions nationwide students are allegedly receiving payments to coordinate anti-Israel demonstrations, lured by promises of substantial financial compensation.

As per an article from the New York Post reports suggest that USCPR, a group supported by Soros is compensating "fellows" to spearhead protests on campuses. The incentives offered range from $2,880 to $3,660 for campus-based fellows and up to $7,800, for community-based fellows.

These individuals are trained to "mobilize for change " dedicating eight hours a week to organizing campaigns supported by organizations.

The depth of Soros influence runs deeper. Since 2017 the USCPR has received $300,000 from Soros Open Society Foundations and an additional $355,000, from the Rockefeller Brothers Fund since 2019.

The ramifications of these protests stretch beyond college grounds. They represent a situation on the brink posing a risk of violence and engulfing the entire nation.

The protests are fueled by an Israel sentiment attracting extremists and radicals who aim to push their own agenda under the guise of social justice. It's not about the protesters themselves; it's the atmosphere of fear and distrust they create that affects every part of society. As tensions rise and sides are taken every day Americans are caught in the middle forced to pick a side in a battle. In these times of civil unrest lets reflect on the wisdom of Abraham Lincoln; "A nation divided against itself cannot endure." It is crucial that we unite as a nation rallying around our shared goals and unwavering in our resolve to surmount any challenges that may arise

This substantial financial support fuels the Israel protests transforming what could have been simple demonstrations into potential hotbeds for violence and unrest.

The depth of Soros influence runs deep $$$

Highlighted as an illustration of how these secretive organizations operate on university campuses is Nidaa Lafi, President of the University of Texas Students for Justice in Palestine. As a fellow with the USCPR Lafi was seen at an Israel gathering delivering passionate speeches and calling for an end to Israels actions in Gaza. It is evident that these protests are not just movements, but meticulously planned efforts aimed at stirring up discord and disunity. The ramifications of these protests stretch beyond college grounds. They represent a situation on the brink posing a risk of violence and engulfing the entire nation.

The protests are fueled by an Israel sentiment attracting extremists and radicals who aim to push their own agenda under the guise of social justice. It's not about the protesters themselves; it's the atmosphere of fear and distrust they create that affects every part of society. As tensions rise and sides are taken every day Americans are caught in the middle forced to pick a side in a battle.

In this situation it's crucial for us to stand together as one nation undivided. We must resist being influenced by groups with motives. Of division and hate we should embrace the values that define us as Americans; freedom, democracy and justice for all.

The challenges ahead won't be simple. The opposition is strong and resolute. We can find strength in knowing we're on the side of history. We need to unite as a people, with a shared determination to create a future for ourselves and future generations.

In these times of civil unrest lets reflect on the wisdom of Abraham Lincoln; "A nation divided against itself cannot endure." It is crucial that we unite as a nation rallying around our shared goals and unwavering in our resolve to surmount any challenges that may arise.

The anti-Israel protests at high-dollar college campuses in 2024 have escalated into contentious displays of activism, marked by arrests and disruptions. Nidaa Lafi, a former president of the University of Texas Students for Justice in Palestine (SJP) and a USCPR fellow, was detained in January for blocking the road intended for President Biden's motorcade during the late Democratic Congresswoman Eddie Bernice Johnson's funeral procession, whom she had previously worked for.

Similarly, Craig Birckhead-Morton, a Yale student and USCPR fellow, faced arrest and charges of first-degree trespassing after the SJP chapter at Yale began an on-campus occupation. Birckhead-Morton's arrest underscores the intensity of the protests and the willingness of participants to engage in civil disobedience to advance their cause.

Moreover, Malak Afaneh, co-president of Berkeley Law Students for Justice in Palestine and also a USCPR fellow, has been actively involved in disruptive actions. Afaneh was among the students who disrupted a dinner for third-year students at the home of Dean Erwin Chemerinsky in early April, showcasing the extent to which USCPR fellows are engaged in high-profile demonstrations.

The involvement of USCPR fellows in these protests underscores the coordinated nature of the activism and the role of well-funded organizations in supporting such efforts. Afaneh's past social media activity, as documented by the Canary Mission, further highlights the ideological fervor driving some participants, as evidenced by her endorsement of the Popular Front for the Liberation of Palestine.

Overall, the anti-Israel protests at prestigious college campuses in 2024 reflect a convergence of passionate activism, organized support networks, and a commitment to challenging perceived injustices. The arrests and disruptions associated with these protests underscore the intensity of the debate surrounding the Israeli-Palestinian conflict and the willingness of activists to confront authorities in pursuit of their objectives.

Chapter 11

The idea of the United States possibly repealing the Second Amendment, which guarantees the right to own and carry firearms is a divisive topic that could potentially spark civil unrest. This important right deeply rooted in culture and history serves as a protection against tyranny and oppression ensuring that individuals have the ability to protect themselves and their freedoms. However, if there were any attempts by the government to remove this safeguard it could lead to turmoil and discord.

The Second Amendment, enshrined in the Bill of Rights, was put in place to prevent infringement on people's rights to self-defense and resistance against tyranny. It acts as a barrier against power being held by the state allowing citizens to arm themselves as a line of defense against oppressive governments or authoritarian control. Throughout U.S. History advocates have vigorously defended the right to bear arms as crucial for upholding freedom and democracy.

The idea of the government potentially revoking the Second Amendment is deeply concerning for Americans since it would signify an erosion of their constitutional freedoms. Such a drastic step would likely face opposition, from those who value their right to bear arms as a part of their identity and beliefs.

The mere hint of such an action could ignite a wave of unrest and opposition among the populace.

If the government were to consider repealing the Second Amendment, it might trigger disobedience and defiance throughout the nation. Many law-abiding citizens, who hold the right to bear arms in regard could choose not to comply with any efforts to take away their firearms. This resistance could result in acts of non-disobedience and even armed opposition against government authorities.

In response to escalating tensions and turmoil the government might resort to implementing law as a means to restore order and suppress dissent. Martial law entails suspending laws and imposing military authority granting broad powers to the government for maintaining control. During law civil liberties and constitutional rights may be suspended, with military forces mobilized to enforce decrees.

The declaration of law could worsen the situation by stoking tensions and encouraging individuals to resist what they perceive as governmental overreach. In this setting clashes between government forces and armed civilians could escalate into conflicts leading to widespread violence and disorder.

Additionally, the participation of bodies, like NATO and the United Nations could complicate the situation further in the conflict. If there were turmoil and civil discord within the United States it might be viewed as a risk to stability and safety. Consequently, foreign entities might step in to ease the crisis and restore order, possibly escalating tensions and escalating hostilities.

To sum up, the idea of America revoking the Second Amendment and trying to disarm its populace is a scenario. Such a drastic move could set off a series of protests, defiance and armed opposition leading to chaos and insecurity. The declaration of law and intervention by organizations could worsen the conflict, dragging the country into a destructive civil war. Therefore, it is crucial for decision makers to proceed cautiously and weigh the repercussions before taking any actions that jeopardize the rights of American citizens.

The looming threat of a war, in the United States in 2024 casts a shadow over the nation risking tearing apart the very essence of society. As tensions rise and political divides deepen the country stands at the edge of turmoil and discord. The lead up to the elections only adds to these simmering tensions with groups competing for power and influence.

Amidst this unrest the presence of United Nations peacekeepers in every city stirs up suspicion and fear among the people. The sight of foreign troops patrolling streets entering homes and confiscating weapons sends shockwaves through the nation raising concerns about government overreach and authoritarianism.

While the United Nations is supposed to be for peacekeeping purposes many Americans view them as a symbol of oppression and despotism. Outraged citizens see it as a breach of their rights and freedoms, leading them to protest on the streets for an end to involvement and a return to sovereignty.

These protests spiral into confrontations, between civilians and peacekeeping forces plunging the nation into disorder and violence. Streets turn into battlefields as opposing factions clash for supremacy.

Amidst the turmoil innocent civilians find themselves caught in the midst of conflict their lives shattered by the devastation of war.

At the time the upcoming presidential elections are overshadowed by the looming threat of unrest. With political parties deeply divided they face challenges in maintaining control over their supporters as the nation edges closer to collapse. The hope for a transfer of power diminishes as opposing groups refuse to accept defeat and resort to measures to retain authority.

In this environment the role of media grows increasingly crucial in shaping opinion and influencing unfolding events. Propaganda and false information spread rapidly fostering distrust and hostility among citizens. The proliferation of conspiracy theories exacerbates divides. Adds fuel to ongoing conflicts.

As violence intensifies and casualties mount, international calls for intervention become more pronounced. However, such foreign involvement only stirs feelings of betrayal and resentment among Americans, who perceive it as an encroachment, on their sovereignty and autonomy.

During disorder and uncertainty individuals are left to fend for themselves as they struggle to survive in a nation fractured by strife.

Families suffer separations communities are left in ruins as our strong nation falls into darkness and hopelessness.

Ultimately the civil strife of 2024 stands as a lesson on how delicate democracy is the risks posed by growing division and polarization. It's a signal of the repercussions of political views and the failure of leaders to mend the gaps that threaten national unity. As the aftermath settles in, the wounds of conflict will serve as a reminder of the sacrifices made for freedom and the vital need for solidarity, in times.

Chapter 12

The end of times, the end of days, and the Mark of the Beast is a popular end-times topic and has been for centuries. More recently, technological advances have sparked more speculation as to what the mark will actually look like and how it will be administered. An intriguing possibility of gaining traction lately is that of an RFID chip.

If you read the Bible, I am sure you have heard about the mark of man, the number is 666. Radio-frequency identification (RFID) uses electromagnetic fields to automatically identify, and track tags (or chips) attached to objects. This technology has been around for decades and currently has many uses such as tracking pharmaceuticals, library books, vehicles, jewelry and other valuables, and wildlife and pets.

RFID allows for the simple locating of these things as well as rapidly identifying them. RFID is the basis for transponder-key vehicle ignitions and contactless payment methods. And now the RFID chip is being used in humans.

Some firms have made RFID chip implants available to their employees; with an implanted chip, an employee can wave a hand to open doors, pay for food in the cafeteria, and gain access to the copy machine.

Proponents of the RFID implants in humans envision a streamlined future in which no one must carry a wallet or a passport, children and the elderly can be located when they wander off, kidnap victims can be found readily, and EMTs can access the medical records of an unconscious patient.

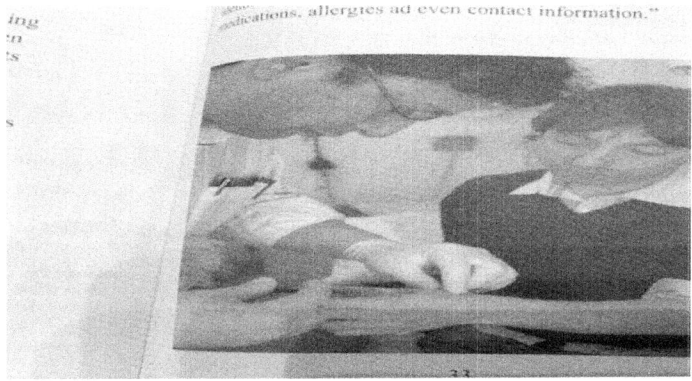

RFID technology in humans is gaining popularity around the globe, but there are concerns medically, technologically, and ethically. For the reader of the Bible, an RFID chip sounds suspiciously like the mark of the beast prophesied in Revelation, especially given that most transponder implants are being placed in a person's right hand.

The book of Revelation gives us some details about what the mark of the beast does. When the Antichrist, or the beast, comes to power, "all people, great and small, rich and poor, free and slave, [are forced] to receive a mark on their right hands or on their foreheads, so that they could not buy or sell unless they had the mark, which is the name of the beast or the number of his name" In mandating the mark, the beast will be able to control commerce and, if it's an RFID chip, track everyone and have access to their personal information. The idea of a conflict emerging in the United States perhaps triggered by the events described in Revelation 13 is truly frightening and thought provoking. In a time when the globe is dealing with upheaval and social discord the looming prospect of war casts a shadow over humanity's future.

As detailed in Revelation 13 a series of events will unfold leading to the enforced application of what's known as the mark of the beast. These occurrences involve the ascent of the Antichrist, to power miraculous healings, widespread adoration for both the Antichrist and Satan and strict measures implemented by a figure known as the prophet. Ultimately individuals will be compelled to accept this mark under threat of consequences.

Although these events are yet to materialize, just contemplating their occurrence sends chills through believers. The mere thought of existing in a world where such horrors transpire is deeply unsettling at best. It serves as a reminder of how fragile civilization can be and sheds light on humanity's capacity for malevolence.

The technology that could potentially facilitate this marks implementation—such as RFID chips—is already present in our world today.

While technology itself is not inherently malevolent it's the misuse of it, for intent that poses a threat to humanity. The concept of people being. Tracked against their wishes, losing their identity and autonomy paints a picture of a dystopian future that we must work to prevent at all costs.

When faced with predictions it's natural to feel fear and uncertainty about what lies ahead. The possibility of civil conflict breaking out as a result of these events only amplifies the sense of unease and unpredictability. The idea of family members and neighbors turning against each other in a struggle for survival serves as a reminder of the destructive force of division and animosity.

Nevertheless, it's crucial to acknowledge that we haven't reached that point yet. The scenarios outlined in Revelation 13 have not materialized, leaving room for humanity to alter its course. Despite the signs of the times there remains potential for redemption and rejuvenation.

As individuals with faith, we are tasked with staying watchful and steadfast in times. It is essential to uphold values such as love, empathy and fairness, amidst chaos and unrest.

By staying strong, in our beliefs and having faith in Gods guidance we can bravely face the challenges of today's times.

To sum up the possibility of a conflict hovering over the United States following the events described in Revelation 13 serves as a reminder of how delicate civilization is and the constant presence of evil, in our world. Nonetheless we should not give in to fear and hopelessness. Instead let us cling to our beliefs and stand unwavering in our dedication to shaping a future for generations to come.

Chapter 13

These days we are living in are the last days! I know something about Civil War and my wife, having studied civil wars all over the world, and the conditions that give rise to them, you argue in your book, somewhat chillingly, that the United States is coming dangerously close to those conditions. Can you explain that?

So, we know a lot about civil wars — how they start, how long they last, why they're so hard to resolve, how you end them. And we know a lot because since 1946, there have been over 200 major armed conflicts. And for the last 30 years, people have been collecting a lot of data, analyzing the data, looking at patterns. I've been one of those people.

We went from thinking, even as late as the 1980s, that every one of these was unique. And the way people studied it is they would be a Somalia expert, a Yugoslavia expert, a Tajikistan expert. And everybody thought their case was unique and that you could draw no parallels. Then methods and computers got better, and people like me came and could collect data and analyze it. And what we saw is that there are lots of patterns at the macro level.

In 1994, the U.S. government put together this Political Instability Task Force. They were interested in trying to predict what countries around the world were going to become unstable, potentially fall apart, experience political violence and civil war.

The looming specter of a war, in the United States is a concerning possibility that many dreads could soon become a harsh reality. While there are conjectures about what might incite turmoil, one prevalent idea revolves around the potential of a racial conflict setting blacks against whites in a disastrous clash of beliefs and grievances.

This troubling situation stems from the enduring tensions and disparities that have troubled society for generations. Despite advancements in rights and social justice systemic racism and bias persistently stoke animosity and rifts among communities of color and their white counterparts. The recent resurgence of white supremacist organizations and the rise in hate crimes only serve to worsen these simmering tensions edging the nation closer to conflict.

Another foreboding theory suggests that the government itself could instigate unrest by orchestrating a catastrophic event, like an electromagnetic pulse (EMP) attack. This speculative scenario entails disrupting utilities and infrastructure throwing the country into disarray and leaving its populace exposed and desperate.

The aftermath of such an assault would supposedly compel people to fend for themselves leading to fear, violence and societal disintegration.
In times of turmoil there is a concern that the government may intervene to restore order and help. However, some are wary that this could be a way for the government to gain control and influence potentially leading to the rise of a regime disguised to maintain security and stability.

The idea of a crisis orchestrated by the government sparking unrest is not unheard of. Historical instances of state-backed violence and oppression both at home and abroad serve as examples of the risks associated with government authority. From operations aimed at foreign governments to quelling dissent within their own borders, governments have frequently resorted to extreme tactics during crises in order to retain power.

Given these scenarios it is crucial for Americans to stay alert and informed about the dynamics shaping their society. Preserving liberties and democratic values should be. Safeguarded against any endeavors aiming to diminish them under the guise of security or convenience. Additionally endeavors toward addressing issues of inequality and injustice must be intensified with dedication to creating a fairer and more inclusive society for everyone.

Ultimately the possibility of strife underscores how delicate democracy is and stresses the significance of remaining watchful against authoritarianism and subjugation.

By remaining aware, involved and unified in times people, in the United States can collaborate to avoid the disaster of internal strife and lay down a path, towards a more promising and harmonious tomorrow.

I didn't do a great job framing it, the whole Civil War Thing, not initially, that when people think about civil war, they think about the first civil war. And in their mind, that's what a second one would look like. And, of course, that's not the case at all. So, part of it was just helping people conceptualize what a 21st-century civil war against a powerful government might look like. The looming possibility of a war, in the United States casts a shadow over the year 2024 which holds significance in its history. With tensions escalating and grievances mounting the nation stands at the edge of a crisis that could potentially divide it.

Insights from the CIAs guide on insurgency suggest that civil unrest typically follows a path progressing through three stages; pre insurgency, incipient conflict and open insurgency. In the insurgency phase discontented groups unite around common grievances rallying support and setting the stage for future actions. Although this initial phase may appear minor with a few individuals expressing their dissatisfaction it lays the groundwork for significant developments.

As dissatisfaction brews beneath the surface the incipient conflict stage emerges as disgruntled factions start to militarize. Militias are formed weapons are procured and members receive training often including ex law enforcement personnel. These groups operate covertly carrying out attacks that are often overlooked or dismissed as events. These violent acts foreshadow turmoil signaling an increase in tensions and the imminent risk of full-fledged conflict.

In the scenario of the United States, in 2024 we are witnessing stages of insurgency that feel all too familiar. The rooted divisions in society worsened by divides, economic disparities and social injustices have paved the way for dissent to grow. Various groups representing ideologies are rallying their supporters, driven by both perceived grievances gearing up for potential conflicts.

The impending risk of unrest is heightened by influences such as the looming shadow of a New World Order. With societal structures weakening and institutions faltering there are murmurs about an agenda aiming to reshape world dynamics with the U.S. Being a target. The emergence of a currency hints at shifts in the global economy that could inflame domestic tensions further.

Amidst this atmosphere of unpredictability and turmoil there is a call for vigilance and awareness. The parallels drawn from the CIAs insurgency manual serve as a reminder of the perils that come with indifference and lack of understanding. Disregarding signs pointing towards escalating conflicts only emboldens insurgent factions. Hastens the spiral into disorder.

Faced with these challenges, it falls upon citizens and leaders to learn from history lessons and take proactive steps to protect the nation's stability and unity.
To prevent disaster, it is crucial to bridge the gap between beliefs, promote communication and tackle the underlying issues causing dissatisfaction.

As we navigate through 2024 the future of the United States teeters on a knifes edge. Will it fall prey to division and chaos. Will it transcend these challenges by working to pave a way towards healing and revitalization? The power rests in the hands of its citizens standing together with a shared goal and unwavering resolve to steer towards a brighter tomorrow.
And so, again, this is part of the process you see across the board, where the organizers of insurgencies understand that they need to gain experienced soldiers relatively quickly. And one way to do that is to recruit. Here in the United States, because we had a series of long wars in Afghanistan and Iraq and Syria, and now that we've withdrawn from them, we've had more than 20 years of returning soldiers with experience. And so, this creates a ready-made subset of the population that you can recruit from.

What do you say to people who charge that this is all overblown, that civil war could never happen here in the United States — or that you're being inflammatory and making things worse by putting corrosive ideas out there?

There are so many words I could say, but there's so many things to say. One thing is that groups — we'll call them violent entrepreneurs, the violent extremists who want to tear everything down and want to institute their own radical vision of society — they benefit from the element of surprise, right?

They want people to be confused when violence starts happening. They want people to not understand what's going on, to think that nobody's in charge. Because then they can send their goons into the streets and convince people that they're the ones in charge. Which is why when I would talk to people who lived through the start of the violence in Sarajevo or Baghdad or Kyiv, they all say that they were surprised. And they were surprised in part because they didn't know what the warning signs were.

But also, because people had a vested interest in distracting them or denying it so that when an attack happened, or when you had paramilitary troops sleeping in the hills outside of Sarajevo, they would make up stories. You know, "We're just doing training missions." Or "We're just here to protect you.
 There's nothing going on here. Don't worry about this."
I wish it were the case that by not talking about it we could prevent anything from happening. But the reality is, if we don't talk about it, [violent extremists] is going to continue to organize, and they're going to continue to train. There are definitely lots of groups on the far right who want war. They are preparing for war. And not talking about it does not make us safer.
What we're heading toward is an insurgency, which is a form of a civil war. That is the 21st-century version of a civil war, especially in countries with powerful governments and powerful militaries, which is what the United States is. And it makes sense. An insurgency tends to be much more decentralized, often fought by multiple groups. Sometimes they compete with each other. Sometimes they coordinate their behavior. They use unconventional tactics. They target infrastructure. They target civilians. They use domestic terror and guerrilla warfare. Hit-and-run raids and bombs. We've already seen this in other countries with powerful militaries, right? The IRA took on the British government. Hamas has taken on the Israeli government. These are two of the most powerful militaries in the world. And

they fought for decades. And in the case of Hamas, I think we could see a third intifada. And they pursue a similar strategy.

In the wake of escalating civil unrest and government overreach, the United States finds itself teetering on the brink of total collapse. As dissent simmers and discontent spreads like wildfire, a shadowy specter looms over the nation: the ominous threat of a real civil war and the imposition of total government control.

Amidst the chaos, whispers of a new mark of the beast—666 chip—send shivers down the spines of citizens already grappling with uncertainty and fear. This dystopian vision, reminiscent of apocalyptic prophecies, sees every individual mandated to receive a chip implanted in their right hand or forehead, marking them as subjects of the regime's surveillance and control. At the heart of this unfolding nightmare lies the concept of leaderless resistance, a strategy outlined in "The Turner Diaries," revered as the bible of the far right. This chilling manifesto serves as a blueprint for subversion and insurgency, detailing how to wage war against a formidable government like the United States without directly engaging its military might.

Central to the doctrine of leaderless resistance is the principle of decentralized action. Rather than confronting the government head-on, insurgents are instructed to disperse themselves across the country, targeting vulnerable sites and evading detection. By operating in small, autonomous cells, they aim to undermine the government's authority and disrupt its control without presenting a clear target for retaliation.

In this dystopian reality, the lines between fiction and reality blur as the nation descends into chaos and anarchy. As the government scrambles to maintain order, dissenters and rebels alike wage a covert war against the forces of tyranny, driven by a shared desire for freedom and autonomy.

Yet, amidst the turmoil and uncertainty, there remains a glimmer of hope—a steadfast resolve to resist oppression and reclaim the nation's lost liberties. In the face of overwhelming odds, ordinary citizens band together, united in their determination to defy tyranny and restore democracy.

As the battle lines are drawn and the fate of the nation hangs in the balance, one thing becomes clear: the struggle for freedom is far from over. In the crucible of conflict, the resilience and determination of the American people will be put to the test, forging a new chapter in the nation's history—one defined by courage, sacrifice, and the relentless pursuit of liberty.

I can't predict when it will occur. It's crucial for individuals to grasp that nations meeting these two criteria and being placed on this watch list face a civil war risk of under 4 percent. While this may seem low it's significant. It implies that with each passing year of maintaining those two conditions the risk steadily grows.

To put it in perspective, consider smoking. If I were to start smoking today my chances of succumbing to lung cancer or a smoking-related illness would be minimal. However, if I were to continue smoking over the decades my likelihood of suffering from a smoking related ailment would become substantially higher unless I alter my habits. This analogy offers a glimmer of hope; we recognize the indicators. Understand that by fortifying our democracy and steering the Republican Party away from being an ethnic group, our vulnerability, to civil unrest can be eradicated. We are aware of this trajectory. Could act upon it. Recognizing these warning signs is essential to instigate change.

Chapter 14

We have been talking a great deal about a potential Civil War, and it is happening right here in the immediate future in the interior of the United States of America. the conspiracy of a small group of powerful individuals working in secret to establish all-powerful control.

The New World Order conspiracy theory becomes antisemitic when it's followed by a reference to a Jewish business leader or political official with a secret agenda who's seeking global control.

A widely used conspiracy theory made popular in the 20th century, the term centers on a cabal of world leaders using the global stage to create an almighty, totalitarian regime that strips people of their individual liberties and consolidates power at the very top.

The conspiracy theory behind the New World Order involving Jewish leaders is based on the idea that Jews have formed a power structure in which they control every aspect of humankind — the economy, media, and political landscape.

I would like to change gears a bit, History shows that the movements to civil and/or international wars that change the domestic and world orders take place via a progression of stages that transpire in big cycles that have occurred for logical reasons throughout history. I believe that reviewing how the typical Big Cycle works, what stage we are in, and what typically comes next is now especially important. That is because the evidence points to us being on the brink of civil and/or international war (in my book *Principles for Dealing with the Changing World Order*, I describe this as late Stage 5, on the brink of Stage 6) and because without understanding how these cycles transpire, we will simply observe events in the news without being adequately prepared for them or able to prevent them.

To be clear, when I say that I believe we are on the brink of civil and/or international war, I am not saying that we will necessarily go into them or that, if we do, it will happen very soon. What I am saying is that the different sides in domestic and international conflicts are preparing for war and if events are allowed to progress as they typically do, there is a dangerously high probability of us being in at least one of these wars if not both in about five years, give or take about three (with the highest risk point being in 2025-26).

War in the USA can happen, while the part of the cycle we are now in has not occurred before in our lifetimes, it has occurred many times before, most recently in 1930-45. For that reason, I believe that now is the time to reflect on how the cyclical cause/effect relationships lead to the progression of events that makes up the Big Cycle, and what we should do individually and collectively to deal with these progressing realities.

One thing I do know for sure, the good thing is that the scary realities are now much more broadly recognized than they were a couple of years ago. The bad things are that a) conditions are deteriorating even faster than I expected, b) the cause/effect relationships and how they progress are not well understood, and c) nothing much is being done to halt their progressions.

So let us go back in time, approximately two and a half years ago, I described what I thought was going to happen, and I hate to say I was right, also i understand *Principles for Dealing with the Changing World Order*. At that time, many people thought the picture I painted—of a cycle that was leading us toward a financial and economic crisis, great internal conflicts bordering on a type of civil war, and great external conflicts that could lead to some form of international war—was implausible and exaggerated. The New World Order is already here people!!!

Now that the financial and economic problems (most obviously the stagflations), the internal conflicts between populists of the left and populists of the right, and the international great power conflicts have intensified, most people see them. Still, most people look at each of these events in isolation rather than putting them in the context of the evolving Big Cycle.

This is concerning because the cycle is progressing quickly, which has raised the odds of moving to Stage 6 (the civil war/war stage) to uncomfortably high levels.

The New World Order works in mysterious ways, the dark, evil, Shadow Governments want to kill the US dollar and make everyone, I mean every man, women and child poor and starving so that THEY can impose their new one world religion onto the entire world with little resistance.

We are now seeing this dynamic occur in most countries with their central banks varying how they are dealing with it. For example, it was most obviously shown in the UK borrowing debacle and less obviously shown in Japan's money printing and devaluation of the yen. In both of these cases—in fact in all countries' cases—the holders of financial assets experienced big depreciations in asset values through some mix of price declines and declines in the value of money.

In those cases in which central bankers are moving more aggressively to raise interest rates and tighten liquidity, that is hurting financial asset prices and starting to hurt the interest-rate-sensitive parts of the economy, whereas in those cases where the central banks are printing a lot of money, we are now seeing more rapid depreciations in the value of their currencies.

Anyways, when the money dries up and all the food shelves have been emptied, Civil unrest will be abundant. To be clear, I am not saying that **civil war or external war will happen**. I am saying that whether or not these wars happen is now too close to call, that we are headed toward them, and that a lot depends on how the leaders and people behave.

In 2024 there is a looming threat of unrest driven by a mix of conflicts involving economics, technology and geopolitics. As tensions rise on fronts the country is caught up in a web of discord, each small battle setting the stage for the next.

The core of these conflicts revolves around five types of warfare; trade and economic disputes competition, battles over resources and investments geopolitical struggles and military confrontations. Although these conflicts differ in nature, they are intricately linked with each escalation leading to the challenge.

From trade disagreements to moving on the stage these disputes heighten in intensity pushing the nation closer to the brink of full-scale conflict. With increasing stakes and blurred lines between allies and adversaries the quest for dominance continues unabatedly shaping history in ways.

The following principles are worth paying attention to when trying to anticipate the outbreak of war:

"The greatest risk of military war is when both parties have 1) military powers that are roughly comparable and 2) irreconcilable and existential differences". "All-out wars typically occur when existential issues (ones that are so essential to the country's existence that people are willing to fight and die for them) are at stake and they cannot be resolved by peaceful means". "The choice that opposing countries face—either fighting or backing down—is very hard to make. Both are costly fighting in terms of lives and money and backing down in terms of the loss of status, since it shows weakness, which leads to reduced support"! "The two things about war that one can be most confident in are 1) that it won't go as planned and 2) that it will be far worse than imagined".

We can see these principles playing out in what is happening in the Russia-Ukraine-NATO war, in the US-China-Taiwan conflict, and internal and external conflicts in Iran, tensions with North Korea, and several less significant conflicts. For example, in the Russia-Ukraine-NATO war, we can see the principles that it won't go as planned and that it will be far worse than imagined at play. This should be a reminder to all countries' policy makers when they think about what their next moves should be now that they are so close to Stage 6.

CHAPTER 15

The American Civil War is sometimes considered one of the most religious wars in modern history. The contending sides each drew from evangelical ideas of understanding the world and their cause; each experienced great revivals in their respective armies; each claimed the Bible for its own side. Abraham Lincoln perfectly captured these ironies in his Second Inaugural Address in March 1865.

Just a little over a month before his assassination, he reflected on how each side had "looked for an easier triumph, and a result less fundamental and astounding. Both read the same Bible and pray to the same God, and each invokes His aid against the other."

Lincoln's perception of the limits of human knowledge of divine purposes was rare. More commonly (though not universally), Americans expressed righteous certainty about how biblical passages applied to contemporary events. These might include the results of the latest battle, the "message" God might be sending in the outcome of this or that event, or the meaning of vast social transformations such as emancipation.

Clergy, laypeople, and soldiers on both sides freely divined God's purposes in history and suggested scriptures to back up their prognostications. On the key issue of slavery and the coming of emancipation, African Americans found in the Bible the clearest connection to the apocalyptic events they experienced. Verses about Ethiopia stretching out its arms to God came to have a special meaning in an age when the war produced the one thing that most whites had little intention of fighting over when the war came: the freeing of nearly four million slaves.

In the spirituals, African American slaves had developed a profound theology of how contemporary lives and events fit into biblical passages and stories. The Bible served one other, grimmer, function as well—to bolster two armies armed with increasingly lethal weaponry. As men learned to place their own actions within a biblical cosmological framework, they also came to understand how crucial their role was in realizing a narrative foretold or sanctioned in the biblical passages. Chaplains carried a similar message to the men in both armies.

Soldiers on both sides, however, most often turned to the Bible for personal encouragement rather than national ideology, as they memorized verses, quoted Scripture in letters, and remembered Bible stories. Ultimately, the battle for the Bible during the slavery controversy and over the course of the Civil War helped to displace a world in which the Bible itself was the primary mode of interpreting contemporary events.

I have explored with subtlety and sensitivity the way Americans thought the Bible supported their side and deprecated the other, even while Abraham Lincoln warned against any such easy providentialism.

 The general history of the American Bible Society provided in Fea 2016 documents how and why scriptures became universally available, even to deprived Confederate soldiers, while the essays collected were priceless to say the least.

Lincoln pointed to the harm that might come from pursuing social reform on the assumption that the reformers were morally superior to those they sought to reform. The lack of sympathy and fellow feeling in such an effort defied human nature and contravened the teachings of Christianity. It thus diminished the likelihood of the reform succeeding and created divisions among fellow citizens. The attitude that Lincoln criticized in the Temperance Address was at least in part responsible for the terrible Civil War that erupted almost two decades later.

Delivered as that war ended, Lincoln's Second Inaugural picks up the theme of the Temperance Address in again calling for reconciliation among American citizens. With numerous references to the Bible, the Second Inaugural moved beyond the rational and natural causes to which Lincoln confined himself in the earlier address, appealing to God's transcendent justice as the source of the charity among Americans necessary to bind the nation's wounds. If we leave judgment, certainly final judgment, to God, then we are left with the admonition to love one another.

President Lincoln

At this second appearing to take the oath of the presidential office, there is less occasion for an extended address than there was at the first. Then a statement, somewhat in detail, of a course to be pursued, seemed fitting and proper. Now, at the expiration of four years, during which public declarations have been constantly called forth on every point and phase of the great contest which still absorbs the attention, and engrosses the energies of the nation, little that is new could be presented. The progress of our arms, upon which all else chiefly depends, is as well known to the public as to myself; and it is, I trust, reasonably satisfactory and encouraging to all. With high hope for the future, no prediction regarding it is ventured.

On the occasion corresponding to this four years ago, all thoughts were anxiously directed to an impending civil war. All dreaded it, all sought to avert it. While the inaugural address was being delivered from this place, devoted altogether to saving the Union without war, insurgent agents were in the city seeking to destroy it without war—seeking to dissolve the Union, and divide effects, by negotiation. Both parties deprecated war; but one of them would make war rather than let the nation survive; and the other would accept war rather than let it perish. And the war came.

One eighth of the whole population were colored slaves, not distributed generally over the Union, but localized in the Southern part of it. These slaves constituted a peculiar and powerful interest. All knew that this interest was, somehow, the cause of the war. To strengthen, perpetuate, and extend this interest was the object for which the insurgents would rend the Union, even by war; while the government claimed no right to do more than to restrict the territorial enlargement of it. Neither party expected for the war, the magnitude, or the duration, which it has already attained. Neither anticipated that the cause of the conflict might cease with, or even before, the conflict itself should cease. Each looked for an easier triumph, and a less fundamental and astounding result. Both read the same Bible and pray to the same God; and each invokes His aid against the other. It may seem strange that any men should dare to ask a just God's assistance in wringing their bread from the sweat of other men's faces; but let us judge not that we be not judged. The prayers of both could not be answered; that of neither has been answered fully. The Almighty has His own purposes. Woe unto the world because of offences! for it must needs be that offences come; but woe to that man by whom the offence cometh![3] If we shall suppose that American Slavery is one of those offences which, in the providence of God, must needs come, but which, having continued through His appointed time, He now wills to remove, and that He gives to both North and South, this terrible war, as the woe due to those by whom the offence came, shall we discern therein any departure from those divine attributes which the believers in a Living God always ascribe to Him? Fondly do we hope, fervently do we pray, that this mighty scourge of war may speedily pass away. Yet, if God wills that it continue, until all the wealth piled by the bond-man's two hundred and fifty years of unrequited toil shall be sunk, and until every drop of blood drawn with the lash, shall be paid by another drawn with the sword, as was said three thousand years ago, so still it must be said "the judgments of the Lord, are true and righteous altogether." With malice toward none; with charity for all; with firmness in the right, as God gives us to see the right, let us strive on to finish the work we are in; to bind up the nation's wounds; to care for him who shall have borne the battle, and for his widow, and his orphan to do all which may achieve and cherish a just and a lasting peace, among ourselves, and with all nations.

ABOUT THE AUTHOR

Meet Huntley, a college grad and dedicated family guy hailing from Indiana. He juggles his love for sci fi and conspiracy theories with the happiness of home life. Blessed with a loving spouse and three kids, he cherishes the joys of biking and frolicking with his four pals.

Even though he's drawn to the enigmatic and speculative Huntley, it stays true, to his roots prioritizing family and community while embodying principles of honesty and integrity in everything he does.

ABOUT THE BOOK

In Civil War 2024, the author Huntley delves into Americas fears painting a vivid picture of a nation, on the edge of chaos. Against a backdrop of unrest looming EMP threats and the secretive plans of the New World Order this thrilling story explores the possibility of another American Civil War.

As tensions rise and society begins to crumble, CIVIL WAR in 2024 provides a haunting glimpse into a future filled with uncertainty and turmoil. From institutions to life on the streets and George Soros funded riots all across America, readers are drawn into a whirlwind of mystery and peril, unable to look away from the gripping suspense.

With attention to detail and a sharp understanding of politics, Huntley weaves a narrative that is both provocative and exciting. A must read for those about our world's future Civil War 2024 is an exploration of the forces pushing humanity to its limits—and the strength of human resilience, in challenging times.

Printed in Great Britain
by Amazon